Introduction to the Immaculata

"Mazrin has presented Our Blessed Mother in one of the most reverent yet approachable ways I have ever read. For those who might struggle with St. Louis de Montfort's work, or those who struggle with the idea of consecrating oneself to Jesus through Mary, this resource will be a game changer. I couldn't recommend it more!"

Chase Crouse
Founder of Hypurofit, Author of *The God of Endurance*

"*Introduction to the Immaculata* is a must-read for anyone who has wanted to learn more about Mary. It is a treasure trove of scriptural reflection and theological insight, and both my mind and heart were drawn closer to Jesus through Mary as I was reading it. I especially appreciate the reflection questions, which work well as a transition into prayer after each chapter, but would also serve as small group discussion points for those who go through this journey with others. Whether you have questions, or even doubts, about the role of Mary in the Church and the world, or you simply want to grow closer to her—this book is for you."

Jonah Soucy
Author of *40 Days, 40 Ways to Pray*

"*Introduction to the Immaculata* by Joshua Mazrin is a beautiful and approachable way to deepen your spiritual life through devotion to Mary. It brings together solid theology, thoughtful reflections, and simple daily prayers to help you draw closer to Christ through Our Lady's intercession. Whether you're just starting out or have been practicing Marian devotion for years, this program offers a meaningful, encouraging path toward living a life totally consecrated to Mary."

Patrick Novecosky

Author of *100 Ways John Paul II Changed the World*

"Joshua Mazrin's model for Marian consecration is like a shimmering gem in the crown of Mary herself. Both theologically enthralling and uniquely accessible, *Introduction to the Immaculata* is an asset to all who want Mary to form them in the School of Love that is her Immaculate Heart. No matter what one's current relationship with the Queen Mother may be, the reflections and practical tools present in these pages will awaken deeper entrustment and set all souls on the path to becoming men and women of 'yes.' Every Catholic Christian should read this book, and 'as soon as possible, as soon as possible, as soon as possible!'"

Cathy Webb

Consecrated virgin and devotional writer for *Blessed is She*

Introduction to the Immaculata

What the Church Actually Teaches
About Mary in 33 Reflections

Joshua Mazrin

St. Kolbe Press is an imprint of the Immaculata Institute.

Paperback: ISBN 979-8-9947739-2-5
E-Book: ISBN 979-8-9947739-1-8

To the Immaculata, St. Maximilian Kolbe,
and all those who helped to found and have
supported the Immaculata Institute.

Table of Contents

Foreword

"Mary, Mary, Mary, this is your life..." So wrote St. Maximilian to himself in his personal diary. There is really never too much of Mary. Nor can there be. Really. It is therefore a joy to see a new book about preparation for total consecration to Mary.

Introduction to the Immaculata will literally lead you into the mystery of Mary, the Immaculate One. You cannot go too far, or too deep. How can that be? Because if you wish to find the King, you should look for Him inside His palace–not just near it, not next to it, but inside, deep inside of it, as St. Maximilian would say. Our Lady is that palace, a living palace, where God has made His dwelling, where He continues to dwell, and where He wants to be found. Do not hesitate to enter, and to go deep. For 33 days you will read about the great things God has done for Mary–the greatest of all His miracles, such a miracle that She approaches as near to God Himself as is possible for a created being (as the Church teaches)–and in the process you will realize, and exclaim with Our Lady, that truly Holy is His name.

But the Immaculata is not a mere object of study, She is a teacher, an all-holy, loving, gentle teacher. As you read you will therefore not only learn about Mary, but you will also learn from Her. If you are feeling the desire to be introduced to Her, it is because She has prayed for you and given you this grace. Do you wish to receive more? I hope so, and that is why prayer will be an indispensable part of reading this book. The Immaculata has a lot to share with you about what God has done for Her, and She will do so if only you ask Her.

What must you do to enter such a profound mystery? Surrender. And this is why: when Our Lord said: "Behold your Mother," He meant it. Mary is really your Mother, who wants nothing more from Her child than unconditional, unlimited, total and trusting surrender. Take Our Lord's words seriously and accept His gift: surrender yourself to Mary, set aside all fear and let Her guide you. And where will She lead you? To God the Father, God the Son, God the Holy Spirit, to the greatest possible intimacy with each of Them.

As happy as I am to see a new book on preparation for total consecration to the Immaculata, I will tell you this: if you are ready now, go ahead and consecrate yourself to Mary at this very moment, before you go any further. I fully agree with the author that you should not wait, and we both agree with St. Maximilian on this. But still read the book. God's works are far too great for our minds to exhaust: you will certainly find something new, something great. That's what happened to me. There is certainly grace, much grace in this book for you as well.

"Mary, Mary, Mary, this is your life." As Mary was life itself for St. Maximilian, I hope She will become your life too.

Fr. Matthias M. Sasko
Franciscan Friar of the Immaculate

Introduction

Devotion to Mary, and even more specifically Marian Consecration, is one of the most beautiful and mystical devotions of the Church. It is a streamlined process to go to Jesus more faithfully, and become conformed to Him, through the powerful intercession of the Blessed Virgin Mary in union with her Indissoluble Spouse, the Holy Spirit.

Honestly, my own interior conversion and the very fact that I practice the Catholic Faith are a direct fruit of Mary's direct action in my life. Many say that Mary is there for the lost causes, the hopeless, the broken, those at rock bottom. Many of the saints and doctors of the Church have said that every saint was made a saint by the Virgin Mary, and that you'd be hard pressed to find a saint who did not have a powerful devotion to her.

If you've ever been to the Sistine Chapel, amidst the other breathtaking depictions, there is Michelangelo's "*The Last Judgment*." Before its restoration, this detail was difficult to make out, but after careful cleaning, it can be seen that angels are pulling souls away from flames by the Rosary. Devotion to Mary not only saved them from damnation, but brought them to our last end: God. In short, the gifts that God gives us through Mary lead us along the progression of the spiritual life—first by helping us overcome our personal sinfulness, and then by further conformity to Jesus Christ, aka, growth in holiness. Mary makes saints, and she makes saints out you and me.

I was certainly on the wrong path as a teenager, but had this unexplainable interior longing for something more. It was the tender hand of Our Lady that reached directly into my life and constantly led me to encounters that personally introduced me to her Son. At first this came through intellectual pursuit, but shortly after she got my butt into the pews, the Lord began a more intensive heart surgery.

This led to a sudden fascination with the Rosary—seemingly out of nowhere. No one was recommending the Rosary to me, I didn't know anyone who prayed it, and honestly, I thought it was for the pious ladies who showed up at 6 am to pray before Mass on Sunday. So I did what any other teenager at that time would do and went to Google "how to pray the Rosary."

I prayed by myself before bed each night and started to feel closer to the Lord and Our Lady in a way I didn't quite understand. But then a friend reached out to me and asked if I had ever done Marian Consecration. I had never heard of it. I ran to the local youth director (who would be embarrassed if I shared his name here), and he told me all about how Marian consecration changed St. John Paul II's life.

After some more research and prayer, I decided I needed to do it, and I needed to be serious about it. I went through St. Louis de Montfort's 33-day preparation for total consecration, and it was intense. It was a whirlwind of a month for me, with many spiritual encounters (both consolation and what seemed to be legitimate spiritual warfare). I realized I had entered into a war that was already raging around me. Truly I hadn't entered it, I was already a part of it, as are you. I merely opened my eyes to see it. Marian consecration was now my way of actively fighting back against the Devil's empty show, as it is Our Lady who has enmity with him, and as St. Kolbe says, it is only Mary who is assured of victory over him. He doesn't like that, so he fears her.

I knew that I was to become a knight in Mary's army from then on. It had truly changed my life forever. Even the day of consecration was a beautiful mystical experience with her and Jesus—having the sensation of physical wind blowing through my body as I recited the prayer, accompanied by a profound peace for which there are no words. It was the presence of the Holy Spirit with His beloved Spouse the Immaculata, making themselves known to me.

Since then, I have fallen in love more deeply with Our Lady and truly found in the spirituality of St. Maximilian Kolbe a deeper understanding of Mary's actions united to the Spirit in bringing us to Jesus. That understanding is precisely why I wrote this book. I wanted everyone to know what the Church teaches about Mary, and how completely necessary a strong devotion to her is for growth in the spiritual life.

So, I set out to write this book which is a combination of an overview of the Church's teachings on Mary, a guide for interior reflection, and a preparation for your own total consecration to Mary. It was originally released as a parish consecration program by the Immaculata Institute, but has been adapted into this book form so more people may come to know what the Church teaches about the Immaculata in a simple, straightforward, and digestible way. As such, you can read this book cover to cover for a quick course on Our Lady, you can read it slowly and devotionally like a personal retreat, you can open to read any topic in whichever order you'd like as they are standalone teachings and reflections, or you can use this day-by-day in order as a method for preparation for total consecration to Mary. Because it was originally released as a tool for preparation for Marian consecration, the first three reflections deal with the topic of Marian consecration before getting into the Church's teachings on Mary. This was not changed because it is fitting that all works about Our Lady lead us toward deeper love for her and her Son, and which is done most perfectly through a total entrustment, or consecration, to her.

Using This Book as a Guide for Consecration

There are a number of other guides out there to prepare for making one's total consecration to Mary, so how is this one different? Well, in short, some of the more traditional models, like St. Louis de Montfort's, is very spiritually deep and enlightening, but can be tough for those who have not read *True Devotion to Mary* or studied Mariology. Other more modern models are very devotionally led, leading you to fall in love with Mary—which is beautiful!

St. Thomas Aquinas, continuing the thought of Aristotle, tells us that in order to truly love someone, we have to *know* them. We have to know God and know the Blessed Virgin to love them—you cannot love what you do not know! Therefore, this model for preparation is a combination of devotion and a survey of the Church's teachings on Mary. It is written in such a way so as to give you a crash course in Mariology, even if you have never studied any theology in your life. The conversational tone helps to present deep and serious topics in an enjoyable, approachable way.

Additionally, this overview the Church's beautiful teachings about Our Lady is presented as a series of reflections, applying each topic to your own spiritual life, and leading you in prayer in response.

For each day, you should begin in prayer, perhaps something simple like the *Hail Mary*. Then read the day's reading, meditate on the reflection questions, and conclude by praying the Marian Prayers found in the Appendix (the *Sub Tuum Præsidium*, the *Hail Mary*, and the *Hail Holy Queen*). When you are ready, it would be helpful to add the consecration prayer of St. Maximilian Kolbe to your daily prayers, as well (it is the formal prayer for our consecration day!).

I am a big advocate for not delaying in doing one's consecration. What I mean by that is, if you are ready today, say the prayer now! Each day that consecration will become deeper, as this is to become a lived endeavor rather than a one-time thing.

I am so pleased that you are joining me and the Immaculata Institute in this preparation and subsequent total consecration to Mary. Marian consecration irreversibly changed my life, and I have one hundred percent confidence if will do the same for yours in the best way possible, if you allow Our Lady to be your guide to her Son.

Day 1

What is Marian Consecration?

"With the act of consecration to the Immaculata we offer ourselves to her as her absolute property. There is no doubt that she is the most perfect instrument in God's hands, while we, on our part, must be instruments in her immaculate hands. When, therefore, will we overcome evil in the most rapid and perfect way throughout the whole world? When we are going to let ourselves be guided by her in the most perfect manner. This is the most important and only issue."[1]

–St. Maximilian Kolbe

Consecration to Mary is one of the most profound spiritual practices in the Catholic spiritual tradition—an act of total trust, surrender, and love. It is the deliberate and

---

[1] Maximilian Kolbe, "1160 Our War," in *The Writings of St. Maximilian Maria Kolbe*, vol. 2, *Various Writings* (Lugano, Italy: Nerbini International, 2016), 2010.

wholehearted entrustment of oneself to the care, intercession, and protection of the Blessed Virgin Mary, with the ultimate goal of belonging more completely to Jesus Christ. Marian consecration is not about replacing devotion to Christ with devotion to Mary. Rather, it is the most perfect and direct way of giving ourselves entirely to Jesus through the one who was most united to Him—His Mother.

When we speak of "consecration," we mean setting something apart for God. In Baptism, every Christian is consecrated to the Lord; we belong to Him. Marian consecration is a deepening of that baptismal consecration—it's a renewal of those promises, but done through the hands of Mary, the one who said the perfect *fiat* ("yes"), "Let it be done to me according to your word" (Lk 1:38). By entrusting ourselves to her, we are allowing her to lead us to the fullness of that same "yes" to God's will in our own lives.

Marian consecration is a way to daily live our baptismal promises—it is a daily renewal of these promises. It is a conscious choice to allow Mary to form Christ in us.

Why Consecration to Mary?

I like to say that Mary is the *magnifying glass* to her Son because her soul magnifies the Lord (cf. Lk 1:46). We can certainly look directly to Jesus, but like trying to read a newspaper with small print, we may miss a few things. When we look to the Immaculata, we actually look through her toward her Son. She magnifies Christ to us. It is through her that we see Him more clearly. That is Mary's entire mission in life: to bring Jesus to us and to bring us to Jesus. Her goal is to magnify her Son and to help us, her spiritual children, become more closely united to Him.

Her will is so perfectly united to God's that all she ever thinks, wills, says, or prays for is what God wants. As such, she perfectly leads us to conformity with Him and His will for our lives. In Genesis 3:15, known as the *Protoevangelium* (the "first Good News"), God tells of a *woman* who will have enmity with the serpent and who will crush his head. The Church continues by saying not only will Mary crush the head of the serpent and be victorious over the dragon in Revelation 12, but Mary is also the one who destroys all heresies in the whole world.

In short, Mary makes way for the truth by eliminating falsehoods. She removes all that blocks our vision of her Son, so that we only see Him. She crushes the head of the serpent in our lives so that all that is holding us back from growing in love with Jesus is removed from our lives—whether these things come from the world, our own flesh, or the Devil.

The One who knows the greatest way for us to come to Him is God Himself. God willed to come to us through this beautiful woman. Through salvation history God prepared His people so that He might become man through this specific Woman. He prepared her like the Ark of the Covenant, making her holy and without blemish. Then on the Cross, he gave her to the Beloved Disciple and him to her—thus Mary is given to us as Mother, and we are called to take her into our homes and hearts. God wills that we come to Him by means of His Blessed Mother. He has bestowed upon her unimaginable graces, making her the surest and most perfect path to Christ—the path that is shortest and even easiest. I don't know about you, but the spiritual life is hard enough already, I fully accept the easier path that leads to greater glory!

Our Path

In the next few reflections, we will discuss what Marian consecration is in greater detail and the different models of Marian consecration given to us by the great Marian saints. We will dive deeper into the richness of devotion to Mary in the Church, exploring the depth of God's love given to us through Mary in ways that apply directly to our own lives. Our program will be a little different, though. St. Thomas Aquinas, echoing Aristotle, said that in order to love someone, you have to know them. As such, our program over the next 33 days will be organized as a survey of the Church's teachings on Mary presented in a conversational manner.

Our goal is that you won't only grow in desire to love Mary, but these reflections will actually teach you about who she is, enabling you to love her with deeper love. Some of the reflections are a little more theological, some present very practical devotional practices, and some speak of beautiful Marian apparitions. We have organized these so that no two days in a row will be too dense, alternating between a Marian dogma and a Marian apparition. We want to learn, but don't want to feel like we're sitting in a classroom. This is why even the more theological reflections are written in such a way that the teachings are applied to our everyday lives as Catholics, trying to grow in love with Jesus through Mary.

I invite you to read these reflections in the presence of Mary and Jesus. Begin with prayer and invite them into the room and your heart. St. Maximilian Kolbe says that when someone reads of Mary, it is not so much the words of the author that matter, but Our Lady will speak directly to the heart of the one reading with the words she wants to share with them.

Reflection

- How do I view Mary currently? What place does she have in my spiritual life?

- Is there anything holding me back from giving everything to Mary? What reservations do I have and where do they come from?

After the Reflection, pray the Marian Prayers the *Sub Tuum Præsidium*, the *Hail Mary*, and the *Hail Holy Queen.*

Day 2

Marian Consecration and the Spiritual Life

"By venerating the Immaculata, we venerate in a very special way the Holy Spirit, and just as grace comes to us from the Father through the Son and the Holy Spirit, so rightly the fruits of this grace ascend to the Father in reverse order, that through the Holy Spirit and the Son, that is to say through the Immaculata and Jesus."[2]

–St. Maximilian Kolbe

Marian consecration isn't just a devotion—it's a way of life. It's not a box to check or a one-time prayer you whisper and move on from, nor should it merely be a mountaintop experience like we experience while making a spiritual retreat. It is an invitation into the deepest transformation possible: to become like Christ, in the school and heart of His Mother.

---

[2] Maximilian Kolbe, "634 To Br. Salezy Mikołajczyk," in *The Writings of St. Maximilian Maria Kolbe*, vol. 1, *Various Writings* (Lugano, Italy: Nerbini International, 2016), 1179.

If you've ever wondered what holiness really looks like, look to Mary. She is the perfect disciple, the one who "pondered all these things in her heart" (Lk 2:19). She is the perfect model of contemplation, obedience, and love. She is perfectly united to the font of all holiness: the Holy Spirit. And that's the goal of the spiritual life: to become holy which leads to union with God.

Mary: The Perfect Disciple

Mary's whole life is summed up in that simple line at Cana: "Do whatever He tells you" (Jn 2:5). She leads us to Jesus with the gentlest firmness—never pushing, never forcing, but never letting go of our hand either.

When we consecrate ourselves to Mary, we're saying, "Teach me to love Jesus the way you love Him." We're asking to borrow her heart, her gaze, her faith. Because let's be honest—our love is weak, distracted, and easily shaken. But hers? Perfectly ordered, perfectly pure, perfectly fixed on Christ.

That's why consecration to Mary isn't about loving her *instead* of Jesus; it's about loving Jesus *with her*. Mary is both the perfect example to follow and the most powerful intercessor who helps us to follow. God has deigned to make Mary the Mediatrix of graces—she hears our prayers as a loving Mother, presents them to her Son, and is united to the Holy Spirit who fills us with these graces. Fathers have called her an aqueduct of grace, a *collaboratrix* with God, and our Advocate. We will explore this more fully in later reflections, but it is a necessary foundation to mention now. Mary is active in our reception of grace if we are aware of it or not.

The Spirit Flies Where She Dwells

Not only does Mary distribute God's graces to us, but she makes way for those graces to penetrate deep within our hearts. As St. Louis de Montfort says, the Holy Spirit flies to wherever He finds Our Lady:

> When the Holy Ghost, her Spouse, has found Mary in a soul, He flies there. He enters there in His fulness; He communicates Himself to that soul abundantly, and to the full extent to which she makes room for her Spouse. Nay, one of the great reasons why the Holy Ghost does not now do startling wonders in our souls is because He does not find there a sufficiently great union with His faithful and indissoluble Spouse. (St. Louis de Montfort, *True Devotion to Mary*)

From the moment of her Immaculate Conception, the Spirit has united Himself to Mary. It is by that action of the Holy Spirit that she becomes "full of grace" (Lk 1:28).

In the quote which begins this reflection, St. Maximilian Kolbe points out that grace comes to us from the Father, through the Son and the Holy Spirit—St. Kolbe has also said, "The Holy Spirit is far too little known." He saw something profound in a way that few others did: Mary and the Holy Spirit are so intimately united that their actions are inseparable. He said that the Holy Spirit only ever works through Mary and that Mary's actions are perfectly united to the Spirit's. They are two unique beings, but live one sole life.

Woah, woah, woah. Let's back up. This is a lot to take in! First let's recall a famous line by St. Athanasius: "God became man so that man might become god" (*On the*

Incarnation). We don't become our own little gods running around lording over things, but by the Incarnation, God has invited us to share in His own life. We begin to live *in* Him. This sharing in God's divine life transforms us, deifies us even, to where, by grace, we participate in God's own life and become partakers of His nature (cf. 1 Pt 2:4).

Mary is the highest and most perfect example of this. By her singular grace received in her Immaculate Conception, her singular vocation as Mother of God, and her singular role in our salvation, Mary is the one most perfectly united to the Holy Spirit. This is so deep a reality that we will have to give it full attention in a later reflection where we break down St. Kolbe's beautiful writings on Mary and the Holy Spirit.

A notable fruit of this thought, though, is that Kolbe said by this same power of the Holy Spirit, through Marian consecration, Mary gives birth to her Son in our souls, as well.

The Spiritual Battle

The saints never tire of saying this: no one enters heaven except through Mary. St. Bonaventure called her the *Gate of Heaven;* St. Alphonsus Ligouri said no one was ever saved without her intercession; St. John Vianney taught that no grace comes from heaven without passing through her hands. Mary is our most perfect guide to her Son, the one who joins with us in our daily battle, who crushes the head of the infernal serpent in our lives.

We do well by accepting and asking for the gifts given by the Holy Spirit which are administered by the hands of Mary "to whom she wills, when she wills, and she wills" (St. Bernardine). We know that we cannot do this alone—we need Our Lady's assistance. Even the gifts that we offer God are laced with our own impurities. The Immaculata purifies our offerings and presents them to her Son as her own as gifts that He cannot turn away, but accepts them with abundant and overflowing love.

When we consecrate ourselves to Mary, we give her all our virtues, good actions, and offerings, as well as our sins, vices, and woundedness. She cleans us up and grants us her own heart with which to love her Son. This is how our true transformation in holiness takes place.

Reflection

Mary's intercession is powerful because of her union with the Holy Spirit. Our consecration to her is meant to be a daily lived experience and volitional offering. Marian consecration becomes our rhythm of life—we give her *everything* without reserve so that she may exercise her full role as our Mother.

- What is keeping me from making my act of consecration right now, and renewing it every day along this preparation?
- How might my days look different if I allowed the Immaculata to have complete control over them?

After the Reflection, pray the Marian Prayers the *Sub Tuum Præsidium*, the *Hail Mary*, and the *Hail Holy Queen.*

Day 3

Models of Marian Consecration

"The first and only goal is the interior life, the attitude of devoted relationship with God, his Mother, and the things of heaven, so as to be her instrumentality in this world and become more like her."

–St. Maximilian Kolbe

As we have said in the previous reflections and is emphasized in our introductory quote today, our goal is the interior life which is our means to union with God. The goal of Marian consecration is likewise growth in our interior life. No matter what model for preparation for Marian consecration, or what terminology is used to describe one's outlook toward it, this remains constant. Total and unreserved consecration to Mary has the singular goal of conforming us to Christ. The way by which we become conformed to Christ is our relationship with Him, which grows precisely through the interior life.

Marian consecration is like hooking up an endless supply of nitrous to the motor that is your prayer life. Mary is the one who pondered all God's mysteries in her heart, and when you consecrate your life to her, she takes you by the hand to lead you deeper into your own contemplation of said mysteries. She helps to pull back the veil so you can encounter her Son intimately and love Him as she does.

With that in mind, there is beauty to be found in some of the different language and the development of this devotion. The language of becoming servants to Mary and entrusting ourselves completely to her is found early in the Church Fathers, but the language of Marian consecration as a devotion promoted to all finds its greatest popularity in St. Louis de Montfort. Following in his footsteps, Our Lady helped her servant St. Maximilian Kolbe perhaps go even deeper.

St. Louis de Montfort

There is a very popular preparation for Marian consecration written by St. Louis Grignion de Montfort, who we may consider the father of Marian consecration in the modern sense. This preparation accompanies his classic book *True Devotion to Mary,* in which de Montfort presents what he calls "holy slavery" to Mary— a term that can sound jarring to modern ears, but in de Montfort's time, it simply yet profoundly expressed a total dependence on the will of God, as Mary herself lived.

For de Montfort, consecration is not a sentimental act—it's a covenant. It is the deliberate choice to hand over to Mary every aspect of one's life: prayers, good works, sufferings, and merits, so that she might purify, perfect, and present them to her Son. In this exchange, nothing of our own remains "ours." Everything belongs to her, so that she may do with it whatever most glorifies God.

De Montfort saw in Mary the most direct, most certain, and easiest route to union with Jesus Christ. Just as she was the chosen means by which God came into the world, so she is the chosen means by which we go to God. To become her "slave of love" is not a loss of freedom but a paradoxical gain—the freedom to belong entirely to God without reserve.

He wrote:

> Oh, how a child, perfumed with the good odour of Mary, is welcome with Jesus Christ, who is the Father of the world to come! Oh, how promptly and how perfectly is such a child united to his Lord! (St. Louis de Montfort, *True Devotion to Mary*)

De Montfort's preparation consists in reading excerpts from *True Devotion, The Imitation of Christ,* Scripture readings, and praying Marian prayers including the Litany of Loreto for 33 days. It is a truly intense preparation that many have described as difficult. Although it is difficult, so is life, and these are instances when we must choose which difficult we want to endure. I would wholeheartedly recommend using de Montfort's method one day if you have not already. After completing our methodology here, you will be equipped with a better understanding of the Church's teachings on the Immaculata and thus de Montfort's consecration will be easier to follow.

St. Maximilian Kolbe & the Immaculata

Admittedly, St. Maximilian Kolbe is my favorite. The Immaculata Institute undertakes the initiative of continuing his work to consecrate the entire world to the Immaculata. St. Kolbe saw Marian consecration as the remedy for all the evils in the world and the means of extending the Blessed Kingdom of the Most Sacred Heart of Jesus as far as possible and as soon as possible. He was a man of great ambition, and after Our Lady appeared to him, he knew his service was to be in her militia.

For more detail on Kolbe's life and his spirituality of Marian consecration, I would have to recommend my book "Led by the Immaculata: St. Maximilian Kolbe's Spiritual Battle Plan for Marian Consecration" which goes through this in greater depth. But for our purposes here, it is important to emphasize that Kolbe went even further beyond holy slavery and considered himself a mere instrument. Although slaves *have to* obey the will of their masters, instruments don't exercise their will at all. They are completely docile in the hands of the one who wields them. This is what Kolbe wanted to be in the immaculate hands of Mary: an instrument at her disposal.

By being an instrument of the Immaculata, one is united to her and to her inseparable Spouse, the Holy Spirit. For Kolbe, Marian consecration was the way to become perfectly filled with, united to, and led by the Holy Spirit. Kolbe said that the Holy Spirit only ever works through Mary, and everything Mary does she does in union with the Holy Spirit.

And the beauty of his thought, is that his way to consecrate to Mary was profoundly simple. Kolbe had no official method for consecration; he said to follow any method you chose so long as you truly gave everything to Mary. In his spirit of boldness, Kolbe would have you not delay, just as I wouldn't. I do not think you should wait until you are done with your 33 days of preparation, I think you should do the consecration now. My hope is that each day you are more and more open, and as you offer yourself to Mary tomorrow, it would be more completely than you did today, and that each day you would more perfectly give yourself to her—that is the spirit of St. Maximilian Kolbe. Do it now, do not delay, do it as soon as possible, as soon as possible, as soon as possible.

Reflection

The model for preparation is less important than truly learning about the beauty that God has done in the Immaculata and what the Church teaches about her, and in response completely offering yourself to her. Our model is meant to help you to know in an easy way what the Church teaches about Mary so that you can love her with greater love. By this we can become holy slaves, or instruments in her hands, with the ultimate goal of becoming conformed to Jesus Christ and allowing Him to live through us.

Beginning in the next reflection, we will discuss God's plan for Mary from the beginning and the Church's Marian teachings.

- Am I willing to give my life to Mary completely now?
- Pray and meditate on the consecration prayer of St. Maximilian Kolbe. If you are willing and ready, pray it now.

Consecration Prayer of St. Maximilian Kolbe

O Immaculata, Queen of Heaven and earth, refuge of sinners and our most loving Mother, God has willed to entrust the entire order of mercy to you. I, a repentant sinner, cast myself at your feet, humbly imploring you to take me with all that I am and have, wholly to yourself as your possession and property. Please make of me, of all my powers of soul and body, of my whole life, death and eternity, whatever most pleases you.

If it pleases you, use all that I am and have without reserve, wholly to accomplish what was said of you: 'She will crush your head' [Gn 3:15], and 'You alone have destroyed all heresies in the whole world' [Office of the B.V. Mary]. Let me be a fit instrument in your immaculate and merciful hands for introducing and increasing your glory to the maximum in all the many strayed and indifferent souls, and thus help extend as far as possible the blessed kingdom of the Most Sacred Heart of Jesus.

For wherever you enter you obtain the grace of conversion and growth in holiness, since it is through your hands that all graces come to us from the Most Sacred Heart of Jesus.

V. Allow me to praise you, O Sacred Virgin.
R. Give me strength against your enemies.

After the Reflection, pray the Marian Prayers the *Sub Tuum Præsidium,* the *Hail Mary,* and the *Hail Holy Queen.*

Day 4

The Protoevangelium: Mary as God's Intention from the Beginning

"I will put enmity between you and the woman, and between your seed and her seed; [she] shall bruise your head, and you shall bruise [her] heel."*

–Genesis 3:15

Immediately following the Fall of Adam and Eve in the Garden of Eden, God began to reveal His plan for humanity's redemption, and right at the heart of that plan is a woman. Just as the Original Sin was done by a man (Adam) with the participation of a woman (Eve), salvation would come by a man (Jesus) with the participation of a woman (Mary). This is not an afterthought, nor is Mary just some "extra" added in for dramatic effect. She was in God's plan from the very beginning, prepared as the New Eve to bring forth the New Adam.

The words quoted above from Genesis 3:15 are known as the *Protoevangelium,* or "first Gospel," since they are God's first announcement of the Good News. Here we see three key figures: the serpent, the woman, and her seed. The serpent is Satan, the deceiver from the beginning. The seed is Christ, the Redeemer who will destroy sin and death. And the woman is none other than Mary, the New Eve, who shares in the victory of her Son over the Devil.

Mary is the one whom God declares would have "enmity" with the serpent—a total, radical opposition. As we will see later on, this is the first proclamation that Mary would be created sinless through her Immaculate Conception.

Mary is Hidden in the Old and Revealed in the New

In the famous words of St. Augustine, "The New Testament is hidden in the Old, and the Old is revealed in the New." With this in mind, Jesus and Mary are found on every page of Sacred Scripture. From Genesis onward, the Immaculata is present, foreshadowed in the Ark of the Covenant, sung of in the Psalms, glimpsed in the wisdom literature, and longed for by the prophets.

Already in Genesis we learn that God had not abandoned humanity to the curse of sin. Our first parents had fallen into Original Sin, and with that came not only death, but concupiscence—the attachment (even an enslavement) to sin. Each one of us, by our own actual sins, adds to this tragic inheritance. We all know this "lot" well: our weakness, our tendency to grasp at things we know cannot satisfy, our pride that resists God's will. Yet right there, in humanity's darkest moment, God pointed to a woman and her offspring as the answer.

In the Fall, we see the disobedience of Eve, who listened to the serpent's lie and grasped at the fruit. Redemption begins with the obedience of Mary, who listened to the angel's word and her response bore spiritual fruit: the Incarnation. As St. Irenæus said, "The knot of Eve's disobedience was loosed by the obedience of Mary. For what the virgin Eve bound by unbelief, the Virgin Mary loosened by faith."

The Enmity Between the Woman and the Serpent

Genesis 3:15 speaks of "enmity" between the serpent and the woman. This is not just a passing hostility, but a total, absolute opposition. Enmity means no compromise, no wiggle room, no middle ground. And if there is to be total enmity between the woman and the serpent, then the woman must be entirely free from the serpent's grasp—that is, free from sin.

The enmity is also said to be between the seed of the serpent (sin) and the seed of the woman (Jesus). As Mary is the most elevated creature, one who is perfect and sinless, she is at the opposition of the most fallen creature, the Devil. Jesus is God, whose total opposition is sin, which is the rejection of God and His Law.

This is the basis for the dogma of the Immaculate Conception, which we will discuss at greater length in a later reflection.

From the first moment of her conception, Mary was preserved from all stain of Original Sin by a singular grace, in view of the merits of her Son. She is the Immaculate One, the one whom Satan never touched, the woman who crushes the serpent's head. This was God's plan from the beginning.

God's Intention of Grace Through Mary

As we have said, Mary is no afterthought. From all eternity, God's intention was to bring grace through Mary. He knew Adam and Eve would fall, and He already prepared the remedy. God went through painstaking detail in preparing the world for the coming of the Messiah, establishing his chosen people and leading them to the land in which He Himself would be born. He established the Davidic Kingdom so the New Adam and New Eve would become the everlasting Davidic King and Queen Mother.

Think about this: before you ever fell into sin, God already provided a Mother for you who would lead you to His mercy. Before you were born, He prepared her intercession to guard you. Before humanity had even tasted death, He already had a plan for the woman whose Son would conquer death forever.

St. Louis de Montfort, the great apostle of Marian consecration, said it this way: "God… willed to commence and to complete His greatest works by the most holy Virgin" (*True Devotion*, no. 15). Creation itself points to this truth: just as all mankind came through Eve, so all grace comes to us through Mary.

Living the Protoevangelium Today

We know too well the effects of sin. Original Sin left us with a wounded nature: concupiscence, suffering, and death. Without Mary, we would be left in this hopeless condition (because God willed to come to us through her). Without Mary, there is no Jesus. But through her, the source of infinite mercy and grace comes to us. She is the living sign that God never intended sin and death to have the final word.

What does this mean for us, concretely? It means that every time we struggle with sin, we should look to Mary. She is the one whom St. Maximilian Kolbe calls *the personification of divine mercy,* since it is through her God brings us every grace of healing and forgiveness in Jesus Christ her Son. Mary's intercession is a weapon—the Devil prowls about like a roaring lion, but she crushes his head (see 1 Peter 5:8 and Genesis 3:15).

Reflection

- How does this change my perspective to realize that Mary was in God's plan from the beginning?
- What are some struggles or sins I just can't seem the shake that I can give to Mary, trusting that she will crush the head of the serpent?

After the Reflection, pray the Marian Prayers the *Sub Tuum Præsidium*, the *Hail Mary,* and the *Hail Holy Queen.*

*The Scripture translation is the Revised Standard Version, but the gender uses St. Jerome's Vulgate which renders this word as the Latin *ipsa,* which means "she," to emphasize Mary's unique role in crushing the head of the serpent.

Day 5

Mary, the Queen Mother

"So Bathshe'ba went to King Solomon, to speak to him on behalf of Adoni'jah. And the king rose to meet her, and bowed down to her; then he sat on his throne, and had a seat brought for the king's mother; and she sat on his right. Then she said, 'I have one small request to make of you; do not refuse me.' And the king said to her, 'Make your request, my mother; for I will not refuse you.'"

–1 Kings 2:19–20

The story of salvation history is intricate yet simple at the same time—such is the work of God. Sometimes Scripture can seem like an unapproachable mountain of complexities, but there is an underlying story that ties everything together, and knowing that underlying story helps us to understand the individual specific passages and pericopes found within its pages.

Scripture is not a random collection of ancient texts entirely written by different authors separated by centuries. Each book has two authors, one human, and the other divine—God Himself. God's inspired Word given to us in Scripture tells a beautiful story of covenants that God made with His people. From Adam to Noah, from Abraham to Moses, from David to Christ, the story is one of family and love, how God calls us to be His children, and as a result, how we make up the Family of God. To explain all this, I'm going to run you through a quick survey of the Bible. This reflection will be a tad longer than others to come, so bear with me and we'll reflect on this together!

The Covenants

The Bible can be read as a series of covenants. A covenant is an extension of kinship by oath. Covenants are not contracts, they do not form merely binding agreements, they form families. By oath, God calls each of us to be part of His family. Adam was not a natural son of God, made part divinity, but God calls him a "son of God." By God's first covenant with Adam, all of humanity was united to God. But we know the story: Adam and Eve sinned in the Garden of Eden and ruptured the covenant.

When they failed, God renewed His covenant with Noah, then Abraham, then Moses, each time expanding the size of His people from a married couple to a family, to a tribe, to a nation, and then through David God established a kingdom.

We can clearly see that God intentionally expanded and formed His people. This work in the Old Testament isn't simply thrown away with the ushering in of the New, it is fulfilled. The Davidic Covenant is very important here, as with this covenant,

God promised that David's throne would be established forever (see 2 Samuel 7:16).

As such, the Davidic Covenant is central, and the Davidic Kingdom's structure is important for us to understand. It was the Davidic Kingdom that prepared Israel for the coming of the Messiah, the one who would rule over all nations, who would be the Son of God, and who would sit upon the throne of David his father forever (see Psalm 89:3, Luke 1: 32–33).

Christ is the Davidic King Forever

When the angel Gabriel appeared to Mary and announced that she would bear a Son, he did so in unmistakably Davidic language:

> 'And behold, you will conceive in your womb and bear a son, and you shall call his name Jesus. He will be great, and will be called the Son of the Most High; and the Lord God will give to him the throne of his father David, and he will reign over the house of Jacob for ever; and of his kingdom there will be no end.' (Luke 1:32–33)

Jesus did not come to sit on the throne of Adam, Noah, Abraham, or Moses. He is the eternal Davidic King who sits on the throne of the Heavenly Jerusalem (a fulfillment of the holy city and central capital of David's kingdom). We even see in Christ's ministry how He founded the Church according to the model of the Davidic Kingdom: He called the Twelve Apostles just as David had twelve officers in his court, one of the Apostles was given primacy over the others (St. Peter as the first Pope) just as David had one prime minister, Christ gave Himself as the Eucharist (which literally means "thanksgiving") just as the *todah* sacrifice was given in David's kingdom as a thank offering to God. All the way down to the queen, Christ fulfilled the Davidic Kingdom, expanding it from an international kingdom to a universal Church.

The Gebirah: The Queen Mother

So what does this have to do with Mary? Well, if Jesus is the Davidic King, then Mary is the Queen Mother.

In the Davidic Kingdom, the queen was not the king's wife, but his mother. The king, after all, often had many wives, but only one mother. The queen being mother to the current king even showed his dynastic succession: that he was true heir to the previous king, his father. The role of Queen Mother was so important that it had a title: *Gebirah*, or "Great Lady."

The Gebirah held a place of honor in the kingdom—she was seated at the king's right hand. In her legal function, the people brought their petitions to her, and she interceded with the king on their behalf. And strikingly, the king himself would bow before her, which he did to no one else: "*The king rose to meet her, and bowed down to her; then he sat on his throne, and had a seat brought for the king's mother; and she sat on his right*" (1 King 2:19).

Mary: Queen Mother and Intercessor

Mary, as the Queen Mother in the eternal Davidic Kingdom, sits at the right hand of her Son, the eternal Davidic King in his heavenly kingdom. She fulfills the role of the Queen Mother by taking our requests and bringing them to her Son who will not refuse her. We have to remember also that Mary is without sin and now glorified in heaven. Her will is perfectly united to that of God's, so everything she prays for she obtains, because she never prays for anything contrary to His will.

She is the most powerful intercessor in all of heaven and earth. Truly, her intercession exceeds even the sum of all other angels and saints since it has been given to her by God the role of accepting our prayers and bringing them before Him as her own. How could Jesus, perfect God and perfect man, the one who follows the Fourth Commandment (to honor one's mother and father) better than anyone else, deny His own Mother? He could not. He has given her this powerful role in heaven as a gift to His people—a gift to us.

The Catechism of the Catholic Church puts this beautifully:

> This motherhood of Mary in the order of grace continues uninterruptedly from the consent which she loyally gave at the Annunciation and which she sustained without wavering beneath the cross, until the eternal fulfilment of all the elect. Taken up to heaven she did not lay aside this saving office but by her manifold intercession continues to bring us the gifts of eternal salvation .... Therefore the Blessed Virgin is invoked in the Church under the titles of Advocate, Helper, Benefactress, and Mediatrix. (CCC 969)

Mary is the true "Great Lady"—she is the greatest Lady of all time. Christ continued to honor her, and has exalted her as God exalts the humble and puts down the proud (See the *Magnificat,* Luke 1:46–55).

Reflection

God prepared His Kingdom with wisdom and order, and in the Davidic Kingdom He established the role of the Queen Mother. Mary fulfills this role in the Kingdom of her Son, seated at His right hand as our advocate and intercessor.

- Do I approach Mary with the confidence of a child who knows his Mother's prayers are heard?
- How can I entrust more of my petitions and needs to her intercession, knowing that Christ the King delights in honoring His Mother?

After the Reflection, pray the Marian Prayers the *Sub Tuum Præsidium*, the *Hail Mary*, and the *Hail Holy Queen*.

Day 6

Mary, Queen of Heaven and Earth

"And a great portent appeared in heaven, a woman clothed with the sun, with the moon under her feet, and on her head a crown of twelve stars; she was with child and she cried out in her pangs of birth, in anguish for delivery. And another portent appeared in heaven; behold, a great red dragon, with seven heads and ten horns, and seven diadems upon his heads. His tail swept down a third of the stars of heaven, and cast them to the earth. And the dragon stood before the woman who was about to bear a child, that he might devour her child when she brought it forth; she brought forth a male child, one who is to rule all the nations with a rod of iron."

–Revelation 12:1–5

When St. John gives us the vision of the Woman clothed with the sun, crowned with twelve stars, with the moon beneath her feet, he reveals something of cosmic significance. This is not just any woman, nor is it simply a symbol of Israel or the Church. She is both those things, yes—but she is also the Mother of the Messiah Himself, who is only one person: the Blessed Virgin Mary, the Ark of the New Covenant.

Bookends: The Beginning and the End

As Scripture draws to a close, God reveals Himself as *alpha* and *omega*: the beginning and the end. These opposing extremes reveal something of His very nature—He is existance itself. Likewise in Sacred Scripture, God uses something called *thematic inclusio*: When something is present at the beginning and end of a particular book or Scripture as a whole, it is meant to demonstrate its importance throughout.

With this in mind, we recall Mary foreshadowed in the Protoevangelium in Genesis 3:15, right as God begins to reveal His plan for man's redemption. Likewise at the end of Scripture, Mary is present as the glorious Woman of Revelation, who appears right as St. John is discussing the return of the Ark of the Covenant in heaven (hint: Mary is the New Ark who appears in heaven!).

At the climax of history, the Woman, now crowned as Queen of Heaven and Earth, is engaged in battle with the ancient serpent as prophesied at the very beginning. The story begins and ends with Mary, because Mary is central to God's plan of salvation, sitting in her rightful place next to her Son who saves us.

Mary and the Battle Against Evil

The image of Mary in Revelation 12 is not serene or passive. She is radiant and crowned, yes, but she is also in the midst of battle. The dragon stands before her, seeking to destroy her Child. War breaks out in heaven, St. Michael and his angels cast down the dragon, and the accuser is defeated by "the blood of the Lamb and by the word of their testimony" (Revelation 12:11).

Mary is not a bystander. She is placed by God right in the middle of the great cosmic battle. Just as Eve stood at the beginning of the Fall, so Mary stands at the beginning of redemption. Where Eve fell to the serpent, Mary crushes his head. Jesus is the only Redeemer, but Mary's "yes" to God made possible the Incarnation of the Savior, and her ongoing maternal intercession strengthens the Church in its struggle against evil.

Pope St. John Paul II taught that Mary's spiritual motherhood is inseparable from the battle described in Revelation:

> Mary, Mother of the Incarnate Word, is placed at the very center of that enmity, that struggle which accompanies the history of humanity on earth and the history of salvation itself. In this central place, she who belongs to the "weak and poor of the Lord" bears in herself, like no other member of the human race, that "glory of grace" which the Father "has bestowed on us in his beloved Son," and this grace determines the extraordinary greatness and beauty of her whole being. (*Redemptoris Mater*, 11)

Mary is Queen because her Son is King, and as Queen she participates in His battle against the powers of darkness.

The Crown of Twelve Stars

John's vision also specifies that Mary is crowned with twelve stars. This points both to the Twelve Tribes of Israel and to the Twelve Apostles—and thus to the whole People of God. Mary is the Mother of the Church because she is Mother to the Head of the Mystical Body.

Mary's queenship is a share in the reign of Christ, extending His mercy to us. As such, Mary is crowned not only as Queen of the Church, but she ought to be crowned within our hearts as queen of our interior lives. What is proper to the whole of salvation is proper to the daily path of holiness. If, due to the will of God, Mary is necessary for Christ's victory over the serpent in Revelation, then she is also necessary for His victory in our hearts. It was God's will to come into the world through her, and thus it is His will that He comes to each of us through her.

We know that for each of us: "we are not contending against flesh and blood, but against the principalities, against the powers, against the world rulers of this present darkness, against the spiritual hosts of wickedness in the heavenly places" (Eph 6:12), and we battle within ourselves against our flesh and the world. We must allow Mary to be crowned within our own hearts so that she may crush the serpent and allow us to overcome ourselves and the world to become conformed to Christ.

As St. Louis de Montfort said in *True Devotion to Mary*:

> In these latter times Mary must shine forth more than ever in mercy, power and grace; in mercy,

to bring back and welcome lovingly the poor sinners and wanderers who are to be converted and return to the Catholic Church; in power, to combat the enemies of God who will rise up menacingly to seduce and crush by promises and threats all those who oppose them; finally, she must shine forth in grace to inspire and support the valiant soldiers and loyal servants of Jesus Christ who are fighting for his cause. *(True Devotion, 50)*

Reflection

How we acknowledge and honor Mary as Queen of Heaven and Earth is by allowing her to be Queen of our hearts. Nothing pleases her more than our cooperation in her work by turning wholeheartedly to God. We allow Mary to exercise this role more fully by our assent and our earnest prayers to her, and by allowing her to take us with all that we are without reserve to be given by her to her Son.

- Do I truly see Mary as central in my daily struggle against temptation and sin?
- How can I entrust myself more fully to her maternal power so that she may crush the serpent's head in my life?

After the Reflection, pray the Marian Prayers the *Sub Tuum Præsidium*, the *Hail Mary*, and the *Hail Holy Queen.*

Day 7

Mary, the Ark of the Covenant

> *"Then God's temple in heaven was opened, and the ark of his covenant was seen within his temple.... And a great sign appeared in heaven, a woman clothed with the sun, with the moon under her feet, and on her head a crown of twelve stars."*
>
> *–Revelation 11:19; 12:1*

The break in between chapters 11 and 12 in the Book of Revelation does not exist in the original manuscripts. In fact, the numbering of chapters and verses came much later. Imagine you are reading this without any numbering—St. John is talking about the Ark of the Covenant appearing in heaven after being lost, and then, all of a sudden, he is speaking of a Woman. This harsh change of subject is in fact no change of subject at all. John deliberately speaks this way to show us that the heavenly Ark of the New Covenant is none other than the Woman herself, who goes to battle with the ancient serpent.

To provide some clarity right out of the gate: the Book of Revelation can be tough to interpret, and these verses in particular mean many things. It is true to say that in one sense the "woman" described refers to the faithful of Israel who cried out for the coming of the Messiah. It is also true to say that the Church is another fulfillment here, who is attacked by the Devil for proclaiming its faith in Jesus.

But the top layer of fulfillment here refers to the Blessed Mother, the only one who brought forth the male child destined to rule all nations with a rod of iron (cf. Rev 12:5). Mary is the true Ark of the Covenant, the Woman of both Genesis 3:15 and Revelation 12.

The Ark in the Old Testament

To understand why Mary is the new Ark of the Covenant, we have to recall what the first Ark was. Built according to God's detailed command (cf. Ex 25), the Ark was the holiest object in Israel. It was a gold-covered chest that held the tablets of the Law, a portion of the manna from the wilderness, and Aaron's priestly staff that had miraculously budded. These three things represented Israel's covenant relationship with God: The Law, the high priesthood, and the manna, all bringing God's presence to His people.

"The Ark was the place par excellence of the presence of God," Fr. Steffano Manelli tells us.[3] It was so sacred that even those who touched it unworthily fell to the ground and died (cf. 2 Sam 6:6–7). It was carried in solemn procession and placed in the Holy of Holies within the Temple, the dwelling place of God among His people. In short, the Ark was the means by which God mediated His presence on earth.

---

[3] Stefano Manelli, FI, "The Mystery of the Blessed Virgin Mary in the Old Testament," in *Mariology: A Guide for Priests, Deacons, Seminarians, and Consecrated Persons*, ed. Mark I. Miravalle (Goleta, CA: Queenship Publishing, 2007), 36.

The Ark in Salvation History

Scripture is filled with typology—where people, places, or things in the Old Testament (types) point to things in the New Testament (antitypes). As we have said before, David's Kingdom is a *type* of the Church, and David himself prefigures Christ. These instances of typology are meant to help us understand God's Revelation and His plan for us.

The typology behind Mary as the Ark of the Covenant is nothing short of exciting, so we will explore a few examples:

1. When David brought the Ark to Jerusalem, he leapt and danced before it (cf. 2 Sam 6:14–15). When Mary, the Ark of the New Covenant, visited her kinswoman Elizabeth, John the Baptist leapt in his mother's womb (cf. Lk 1:41).
2. David asked, "How can the Ark of the Lord come to me?" (cf. 2 Sam 6:9). Elizabeth asked, "And why is this granted me, that the mother of my Lord should come to me?" (Lk 1:43).
3. David brought the Ark into the house of Obed-edom and then went into Jerusalem (cf. 2 Sam 6:2; 10–11). Mary arose and went in haste into the hill country to a city of Judah (cf. Lk 1:39). Mary passed through the same exact geographical location and likewise with haste. Scripture intentionally uses the same language.
4. The Ark remained in the house of Obed-edom for three months, bringing blessing (cf. 2 Sam 6:11). Mary remained with Elizabeth for three months, bringing blessing (cf. Lk 1:56).
5. The Ark was overshadowed by the glory cloud of God's presence (cf. Ex 40:35). Mary was overshadowed by the Holy Spirit, conceiving the Son of God (cf. Lk 1:35)—again the same specific language is used.

These are not accidental or coincidental. The Holy Spirit inspired Luke and John to write in such a way that clearly expressed Mary as the New Ark.

Mary Fulfills the First Ark

The Blessed Virgin Mary is truly the fulfillment of the first Ark, because she carried the fulfillment of each of the things contained within the first Ark. She did not merely carry the Word of God inscribed upon stone tablets, but the Word of God made flesh. She did not only carry the staff of Aaron which represented the priesthood, but the Eternal High Priest Himself. She did not only carry the manna that came down from heaven, but the true Bread of Life which would be given up for us, that which we receive at each Mass in the Eucharist: God Himself.

The Ark was holy because it made present the invisible God. In the same way, Mary is holy because of her vocation to bear God Incarnate. She was preserved from all stain of Original Sin just as the Ark was beautifully built and overlaid with gold to be a fitting vessel for God's presence.

Through Mary, "the Word became flesh and dwelt among us" (John 1:14). Mary's entire role is to mediate God to us. This is clearly seen when she begins her apostolate by bringing Christ to Elizabeth, who became filled with the Holy Spirit at the sound of Mary's greeting, and resulting in the yet-to-be-born John the Baptist leaping in the womb.

Reflection

Just as Israel had to draw near to the Ark to encounter God's presence, so we must draw near to Mary. Drawing near to Mary is like entering the Holy of Holies—the closer we get to

Mary, the more powerfully we will be immersed in the overshadowing presence of God.

- How has this reflection changed my perspective on Mary's role in my own salvation and in my prayer life?
- How can I draw nearer to Mary so that she may bring me deeper into the presence of Christ?

After the Reflection, pray the Marian Prayers the *Sub Tuum Præsidium,* the *Hail Mary,* and the *Hail Holy Queen.*

Day 8

The Visitation: Mary Mediates God's Presence

"In those days Mary arose and went with haste into the hill country, to a city of Judah, and she entered the house of Zechari'ah and greeted Elizabeth. And when Elizabeth heard the greeting of Mary, the child leaped in her womb; and Elizabeth was filled with the Holy Spirit."

–Luke 1:39–41

The mystery of the Visitation is more than just a touching story about two pregnant relatives meeting. In reality, it is one of the clearest demonstrations in Scripture of Mary's unique role in salvation history: she mediates the presence of God. Just as the Ark of the Covenant brought the presence of the Lord to His people in the Old Testament, so Mary, the Ark of the New Covenant, brings Christ Himself into the home of Elizabeth and Zechariah.

Mary as the New Ark Which Brings the Presence of God

Recall from the reflection on Mary as the New Ark of the Covenant: the Old Testament Ark was carried into the hill country of Judah to the house of Obed-edom, where it remained for three months, bringing blessing (cf. 2 Sam 6:11). Luke tells us that Mary also traveled, "into the hill country, to a city of Judah" and remained with Elizabeth "about three months" (cf. Lk 1:56). This parallel is unmistakable, a clearly intentional example of typology that Luke wants his readers to notice. The old Ark mediated God's presence in a shadow; Mary mediates His presence physically.

Think of how intentionally God instructed his people to construct the Ark of the Old Testament, how the Ark itself was holy and central to bringing God's presence to His people. This has also been God's intention for Mary from the beginning, that she be the New Ark which brings salvation to God's people by mediating His presence and bringing them their Redeemer. Mary, too, is holy because of her unique creation, fit to become the New Ark. This holiness is granted to her in her Immaculate Conception, whereby she was preserved from all stain of Original Sin and united so perfectly to the Holy Spirit.

The Mother of My Lord

Also striking is Elizabeth's response to Mary: "And why is this granted me, that the mother of my Lord should come to me?" (Lk 1:43). Modern readers may simply assume that Elizabeth knew that Mary was carrying the Messiah and chose to call Him "Lord" out of reverence to Him, and while beautiful, that interpretation misses a key point.

In the Davidic Kingdom, as we have read, the queen is the mother of the king rather than his wife. This Queen Mother—the Gebirah ("Great Lady")—was referred to by the title "mother of my Lord." So when Elizabeth is calling her kinswoman Mary the "mother of my Lord" she is really addressing her as the Queen Mother of the Davidic Kingdom, the one who bears the child who will be the eternal Davidic King.

Likewise, Elizabeth's words are filled with awe, and echo the words of David when the Ark of the Old Covenant came to him: "How can the ark of the Lord come to me?" (2 Sam 6:9). The words so carefully chosen by Luke and inspired by the Holy Spirit are meant to convey that in Mary's visitation to Elizabeth, she is clearly being called the New Ark of the Covenant and the Queen Mother of the kingdom.

The Joy of the Holy Spirit

The parallels to David and the Ark in the Old Testament do not stop there. In the Old Testament, David danced with all his might before the Ark (cf. 2 Sam 6:14). Luke is careful to point out that likewise when the Ark was brought before the one who was to announce the way of the Lord, St. John the Baptist, leaped in the womb (or danced, if you will) at the sound of Mary's greeting (cf. Lk 1:45).

It is the moment that the sound of Mary's greeting came to Elizabeth's ears that she was filled with the Holy Spirit (cf. Lk 1:41). In other words, God works through Mary to pour out His Spirit. Already we see foreshadowed what countless saints and Doctors of the Church would later teach: devotion to Mary and consecration to her is the surest way to receive the fulness of the Holy Spirit.

This is why St. Louis de Montfort could say that when the Holy Spirit finds Mary in a soul, He rushes there, because she is His inseparable spouse. From the very first pages of Luke's Gospel, the Spirit and Mary are shown to work together to bring Christ to the world.

Mary, the Mediatrix of Christ's Presence

The Visitation is not simply a historical event; it is a model of what Mary continues to do. Wherever she goes, she carries Christ. Wherever she is welcomed, the Spirit is poured out. Whenever she is acknowledged as Queen Mother, Jesus is exalted as King.

This is why the Church calls her *Mediatrix*. Not because she stands between us and Christ as a rival, but because she brings Christ to us most perfectly. Just as the Ark was the means God Himself established to be present to His people, so Mary is the living Ark God Himself has given us.

The Catechism expresses this truth beautifully:

> This motherhood of Mary in the order of grace continues uninterruptedly from the consent which she loyally gave at the Annunciation and which she sustained without wavering beneath the cross, until the eternal fulfillment of all the elect. Taken up to heaven she did not lay aside this saving office but by her manifold intercession continues to bring us the gifts of eternal salvation. ... Therefore the Blessed Virgin is invoked in the Church under the titles of Advocate, Helper, Benefactress, and Mediatrix. *(CCC 969)*

In other words, Mary is our Mother who continues to bring us God's presence through her intercession—she is the Mediatrix of graces because it is through her that Jesus comes to us, and all grace is given to us from Him.

Reflection

The Visitation reveals Mary as the Ark of the New Covenant, the Queen Mother, and the Mediatrix of both Christ's presence and the presence of the Holy Spirit.

- Do I welcome Mary into my home and heart with the same reverence Elizabeth did?
- Do I acknowledge her as the Mother of my Lord, the Queen Mother of the Kingdom, the Church?
- Am I open to the Holy Spirit who is always present with Mary?

After the Reflection, pray the Marian Prayers the *Sub Tuum Præsidium*, the *Hail Mary*, and the *Hail Holy Queen.*

Day 9

Marian Devotion in the History of the Church

"When Jesus saw his mother, and the disciple whom he loved standing near, he said to his mother, 'Woman, behold your son!' Then he said to the disciple, 'Behold your mother!'"

–John 19:26–27

From the very moment Jesus gave Mary to John the Beloved Disciple at the foot of the Cross, Marian devotion became a living reality in the heart of the Church. Jesus found it of such importance, that this interaction is one of only seven things Christ said from the Cross. This was not merely a sentimental gesture by Christ ensuring His Mother would be cared for. No—this was a deliberate, theological act. Jesus was saying to all of us: Mary, the Mother of God is the Mother of all the faithful. As such, we are all her children—she is the Mother of the Church.

The first act of Marian devotion began not in the catacombs, not in the hymns of the Fathers, not in medieval monasteries, but at the foot of the Cross, where the Church was born from the side of Christ, where Mary was given to us as our spiritual Mother in the way of grace.

From that moment, every authentic devotion to Mary is a participation in the filial relationship John received that day. We stand in John's place as Christ's disciples beloved by Him, and we receive the same command: *Ecce Mater tua*—Behold your Mother! And like John, we must take her "into *our* own" (cf. Jn 19:27)—into our homes, into our parishes, and into our hearts.

The Early Church and the Mother of the Lord

In the early centuries of Christianity, during times of great persecution, Christians gathered in the Roman catacombs to pray. It is here that we find some of the earliest depictions of Mary. She is often portrayed with the Child Jesus, a sign of the Incarnation which she made possible through her *fiat*. The earliest Christians turned their gaze to her not only as the one who gave birth to Christ, but also as the living icon of the Church: she who bore Christ in her body shows us what it means to bear Him in our lives. She is the image of conformity to God and His will that we seek to emulate in our own lives.

It is here that we find the oldest Marian prayer we have, the *Sub Tuum Praesidium*, which dates back to the third century. The words are simple yet powerful:

> *We fly to your protection, O Holy Mother of God; despise not our petitions in our necessities, but deliver us always from all dangers, O glorious and blessed Virgin.*

This is no small thing. At a time when Christians were hiding underground, facing martyrdom, and clinging to the faith in the face of Roman power, they instinctively turned to Mary for protection. They believed in her intercession, her maternal care, her closeness to Christ. Notice how the prayer appeals to her not as a distant figure, but as one whose protection is immediate and powerful. This is Marian devotion at its most basic: in danger, in trial, in daily need, the Church turns instinctively to her Mother.

Mary in the Fathers of the Church

Mary has been present in the teachings of the Church from the very beginning. Take, for instance, St. Ephrem the Syrian (4th century), who wrote hymns filled with praise for Mary and her role in salvation history: "You alone and Your Mother are more beautiful than the others, for there is no blemish in You, nor any stains upon Your Mother." St. Ephrem saw in Mary the perfect mirror of her Son's holiness—the one most closely united to Him and most radiant with His grace. Far from obscuring Christ, her purity reveals Him; far from distracting from the Redeemer, she magnifies Him.

Likewise consider St. Augustine, who, according to Louis de Monrtfort, described Mary as the "mold of God." With this in mind, we recall that as the goal of the Christian life is to become holy, like Christ, Mary is the most perfect model and aid in our sacred task. St. Louis de Montfort gave us a telling analogy: when a sculptor wants to make a slab of marble into a beautiful sculpture, he hammers and chisels away bit by bit with strikes and blows. We can be formed in this likeness to Christ by having our sinfulness chipped away and stricken off, but it is often laborious and painful. Another way to create a likeness is to use a mold. Mary is this mold for us to become like

Christ. Instead of being chiseled, we can be melted down by the fire of God's love and placed into the mold, Our Lady, who makes us like her Son.

Mary as the New Eve

In addition to these, many of the early Fathers referred to Mary as the "New Eve," emphasizing that Mary was created utterly equal to Eve (without Original Sin), but was given the special graces for her vocation to become the Mother of God. Then Mary, through her obedience to God's will, untied the knot created by Eve's disobedience. We will explore this title in more detail in the next reflection.

The Beginning of Marian Consecration

With the growing devotion in the Early Church, many Fathers and Doctors of the Church saw that the easiest way to become united to God is through that very "mold" of which we just spoke. Alphonsus of Toledo in the 7th century declared himself to be the servant of the Handmaid of the Lord, because Our Lady is the Mother of the Lord. Pope John VII in the 8th century went even further, calling himself a slave of the Mother of God, a phrase echoed by St. Anselm (11th century) and St. Bernard of Clairvaux (12th century), as well. Bernard tells us to commend everything to Mary, whatever we offer.

Reflection

Mary has been venerated and loved by the faithful from the very beginning of the Church. Her role as our Mother was not an afterthought, but part of God's plan revealed on Calvary and lived out by the first Christians. As we will see in the coming reflections, the Church's early teachings on Mary were always meant to provide clarity on her understanding of God, and to lead us closer to Jesus Christ.

- How can I more intentionally "Behold your Mother" and take her into my home and heart?
- Reflect upon the *Sub Tuum Praesidium*. How can I emulate the early Christians who turned to Mary in all things, especially in the context of great troubles?

After the Reflection, pray the Marian Prayers the *Sub Tuum Præsidium*, the *Hail Mary*, and the *Hail Holy Queen.*

Day 10

Mary as the New Eve

"The knot of Eve's disobedience was loosed by the obedience of Mary. For what the virgin Eve had bound fast through unbelief, this did the virgin Mary set free through faith."

–St. Irenæus of Lyons, Against Heresies

One of the earliest and most powerful titles given to Our Lady is the *New Eve*. This title did not arise in the Middle Ages or from later Marian piety, but from the very earliest centuries of the Church. The Fathers of the Church, reflecting deeply on Scripture and the mystery of salvation, recognized from the beginning that the work of Christ, the New Adam, was inseparably tied to the role of Mary, the New Eve.

Why does this matter? Because it reveals that devotion to Mary is not a pious "add-on," but part of the very structure of salvation. From the dawn of creation, through the tragedy of the Fall, and into the fullness of redemption in Christ, Mary has been part of God's plan.

The Fall Through a Man and a Woman

The book of Genesis tells us that the Fall took place by the action of a man, Adam, with the participation of a woman, Eve, and involved a tree, the Tree of Knowledge of God and Evil. Adam did not fulfill his obligation to guard the Garden of Eden and protect his bride. Eve was not entirely passive in this, she listened to the serpent, doubted God's command, and gave the fruit to her husband.

We see how God flips the script by taking the same characters—a man, a woman, and a tree—to redeem His people. Our redemption came by way of a man, Jesus—the New Adam who in an act of perfect obedience protects all of mankind, rescuing them from sin. But He does not do this alone, there is also the participation of the "woman," Mary—the New Eve. She is also not passive, but instead of saying "no" to God, she says "*fiat*"— "Let it be done to me according to your word" (Lk 1:38). This action of man and woman also involves another tree, the one which becomes to Tree of Life: the Cross.

Mary provides for us the perfect example of participating in God's plan and following His will. It is the simple, yet often difficult task of saying "fiat" in our own lives. The entrance to the path of holiness is saying "yes" to God, and Mary is the ultimate example of someone whose entire life is a "yes" to God's will without any reservation.

The New Eve in the Church Fathers

The early Fathers of the Church spoke clearly about this mystery. St. Justin Martyr in the second century wrote:

> For Eve, being a Virgin and undefiled, conceiving the word that was from the serpent, brought forth disobedience and death; but the

> Virgin Mary, taking faith and joy, when the Angel told her the good tidings, that the Spirit of the Lord should come upon her and the power of the Highest overshadow her. (*Dialogue with Trypho*)

And Irenæus adds:

> Mary the Virgin is found obedient, saying, Behold Thy handmaid, O Lord; be it to me according to Thy word. But Eve was disobedient; for she obeyed not, while she was yet a virgin. As she, having indeed Adam for a husband, but as yet being a virgin … becoming disobedient, became the cause of death both to herself and to the whole human race, so also Mary, having the predestined man, and being yet a Virgin, being obedient, became both to herself and to the whole human race the cause of salvation. (*Against Heresies*)

For the Fathers, the New Adam and the New Eve stand side by side. Jesus is the Redeemer, but Mary's role is real. As Eve was "mother of all the living" in the order of nature, so Mary becomes the spiritual Mother of all the living in the order of grace.

Notice something important here: the Fathers are not speaking with hesitation. They do not say, "perhaps Mary is something like Eve." They proclaim with certainty that Mary is the New Eve. This is the seed of all later Mariology and important for each of our spiritual lives, because it shows us that God planned from the beginning to involve Mary in our redemption.

God Respects Our Free Will

As St. Augustine told us, "God created us without us, but He did not will to save us without us." Our free will is essential to our own salvation. God does not force His grace upon us, and neither does His Mother. Eve chose freely to mistrust God. Mary chose freely to believe. Eve grasped at the fruit in disobedience. Mary opened her hands in surrender: "Be it done unto me according to your word."

This principle is at the very heart of entrusting ourselves to Mary—consecration to Mary. God has entrusted us to her maternal care, and her role is real. But she will not force her hand upon us. Just as God respects our freedom, so too does the Immaculata. She more fully exercises her maternal role in our lives the more we give her permission.

It is through Mary that Jesus comes to us, and it is through Mary that we return to Jesus. Knowing this allows us to "get out of the way" or "get with the program," so that cooperating with this, we open ourselves to every grace offered to us by God.

The more we acknowledge Mary for who she is, and the roles God has given her, the greater permission we give her to exercise those roles in our lives. By this, Mary continues the mission she has: to bring us to her Son and help us to become more deeply united to Him by the power of the Holy Spirit. All Mary wants us for us to grow more deeply in love with her Son.

Reflection

God Himself waited for Mary's *fiat* to bring the Savior into the world. He chose not to act without her consent. In the same way, Our Lady waits for our *fiat* so that we may be more perfectly open to Christ.

- In what areas of my life do I still hesitate to give a full "yes" to God and to the Immaculata?
- How does Mary's role as the New Eve inspire me to trust God's plan for my life more completely?

After the Reflection, pray the Marian Prayers the *Sub Tuum Præsidium*, the *Hail Mary*, and the *Hail Holy Queen*.

Day 11

Mary—The Mother of God

"The Holy Spirit will come upon you, and the power of the Most High will overshadow you; therefore the child to be born will be called holy, the Son of God."
–Luke 1:34

One of the most foundational truths about Mary is expressed in the first of the Church's four Marian dogmas: she is Mother of God (Theotokos). All that Mary is emanates from this reality—she is the one chosen by God to become the Mother of God. As we will later learn, her Immaculate Conception is a special grace given to her in view of this vocation. It is because of this vocation that God chose to bless her in ways almost unimaginable, which are certainly a mystery beyond our total comprehension.

The purpose of our text is, of course, to draw us into deeper love and devotion to Our Lady, and to allow her into our lives more fully, we have to learn more about her in order to love her. As such, we will be exploring each of the four Marian dogmas of the Church so this foundation can help us to learn more about who she is in our own spiritual lives. These reflections may be a little more theologically dense but will provide a window to peer into God's mysteries and allow us to ponder and meditate upon their truths more deeply.

The title Mother of God is not a matter of abstract devotion, but it is a precise theological proclamation which helps us not only to understand who Mary is, but who Jesus is. All teachings on Mary help us to know God—this is her whole mission. This is also why the Church says of Our Lady, "you alone have destroyed all the heresies in the whole world" (Office of the Blessed Virgin Mary).

Mary is the Mother of God so that Christ might truly become one of us, fully divine and fully human. By saying "yes" to God, Mary became the living bridge through which the eternal Word entered creation.

The Significance of the *Theotokos*

The title *Theotokos* literally translates to "Bearer of God," but is frequently used to reference Mary as the Mother of God. In the 3rd century, the devotional use of this title began to spread. There was one bishop, however, that had an issue with it: Nestorius was willing to call Mary the *Christotokos* ("Bearer of Christ") but was not willing to call her Theotokos. His reasoning was that Mary could not be the Mother of God because God existed before her and created her. This is a line of thought that is less common today, but you might hear it said in some non-Catholic circles.

Nestorius believed that Mary was mother Jesus' humanity, but not his divinity. What this meant for him, though, was that Jesus was a union of two different persons: human and divine. A mother is not the mother to a nature, but to a person. Think of your own mother, for example, she is not merely the mother of your humanity or your human nature, she is your mother. You are a person.

The Church knew there was a problem with Nestorius's views, so the Ecumenical Council of Ephesus was called in 431. St. Cyril of Jerusalem came to bat in defense of the title Theotokos, arguing that Jesus was not two different persons, but one divine Person with two natures. His two natures, human and divine, are united perfectly to one another in something called the *hypostatic union*.

This was later clarified even further at the Ecumenical Council of Chalcedon in 451, which said that Christ's natures are united without separation, change, confusion, or division. This means that Jesus' human and divine natures are perfectly united to each other forever—they can never be separated; the union does not change either nature—the divine nature doesn't squash or alter the human nature and the human nature doesn't lessen the divine nature; there is a clear distinction between the two natures—the divine nature doesn't absorb the human nature; and they do not divide the person into two persons, but exist in one subject: Jesus Christ.

Now it's OK if you need to go back and re-read that! But see how this little title of Mary, which teaches us about the beauty of God's plan carried out in Our Lady, teaches us even more about her Son. We see more clearly that Jesus is one Person, and the union of his natures make Him truly God and truly man. God the Son has always been God, but at the moment of the Incarnation, He took on a human nature which is united to His divine nature—He is one Person with two natures. It is by this that Jesus is the true Mediator, the one who unites God with man at the deepest level. And Mary participates in this by bringing God to us in the flesh.

A simple way to summarize the title Theotokos is called the *communication of idioms*. We have already said that a mother is a mother to a person rather than to a nature. So, if Mary is the Mother to the Person Jesus Christ, and Jesus Christ is God, then therefore Mary is the Mother of God. She is the mother of the Son in his humanity, she did not bring his divinity into existence, but she is still rightly the Mother of the Person. This is similarly expressed when St. Peter said to the Jewish authorities, "you…killed the Author of life" (Acts 3:15). By this Peter is saying that they killed God—but of course Jesus died only in His humanity, His divinity didn't die. Still, we rightly say that He died—it is the Person who dies, and in this case He died in His humanity.

Mary's title as Mother of God is therefore inseparable from the truth about Jesus. To honor Mary as Theotokos is to honor the Incarnation and to safeguard the unity of Christ's two natures.

Reflection

Understanding Mary as Mother of God reminds us of the purpose of Marian devotion: to draw closer to Christ. She is the surest guide to Him, the first disciple, and the Mother of the Church who teaches us how to participate in God's plan.

- How do I recognize Mary's role in my own spiritual life—as Mother, as guide, as intercessor?
- In what ways might a deeper understanding of Mary as Mother of God increase my love for Christ and trust in His plan?
- How can I allow her maternal guidance to shape my prayer, devotion, and discipleship?

After the Reflection, pray the Marian Prayers the *Sub Tuum Præsidium,* the *Hail Mary,* and the *Hail Holy Queen.*

Day 12

Our Lady of Guadalupe

"Am I not here, I who am your Mother?"
– Our Lady to St. Juan Diego, 1531

Sometimes devotion grows not just through meditation on Scripture or theology, but through encountering Mary in the living history of the Church. One of the most striking examples is Our Lady of Guadalupe, whose apparition to St. Juan Diego in 1531 continues to inspire devotion and conversion around the world, particularly in the Americas, where Our Lady of Guadalupe is venerated as the *Patroness of the Unborn.*

In December of 1531, Mary appeared multiple times to Juan Diego, a humble indigenous man in Mexico. She spoke to him in his own language, Nahuatl, and asked that a church be built in her honor on the hill of Tepeyac. Despite initial skepticism from the local bishop, her presence was confirmed through a miraculous sign: roses blooming out of season and, most famously, the image of Mary miraculously imprinted on Juan Diego's tilma, or cloak.

Historical Context

The apparition of Our Lady of Guadalupe took place at a pivotal moment in human history. Only a decade earlier, the Aztec Empire had fallen, bringing an end to a civilization steeped in ritual violence. The native peoples of Mexico lived under the shadow of a religion that demanded continual human sacrifice—tens of thousands of victims offered to false gods in hopes of sustaining the sun and ensuring fertility. This was not merely a cultural practice, but a profound spiritual darkness. In 1487, in honor of the Aztecs' reconsecration of their Great Pyramid of Tenochtitlan, 80,000 human beings were sacrificed, with their hearts removed from their bodies and piled up to be offered in sacrifice.

Yet when the Spanish arrived in 1519, they brought the Cross of Christ along with their conquest of the Aztec people. But even with the Gospel proclaimed, the wounds of war left many confused, fearful, and hurt. It was into this world, wounded yet yearning for truth, that the Mother of God appeared.

In 1531, only 44 years after the massive human sacrifice, Our Lady appeared to Juan Diego to heal these wounds. She appeared as a young Aztec-looking woman, wearing a garb familiar to the people. She wore feathers and symbols Juan Diego would have recognized, and spoke his language. Our Lady meets us where we are, meeting us with the same words she spoke to Juan Diego, "Am I not here, I who am your Mother?"

The Story of the Apparitions

On the cold morning of December 9, 1531, Juan Diego was walking across Tepeyac Hill outside Mexico City on his way to Mass. As dawn broke, he heard the sound of heavenly music—sweet birdsong that stilled the air. Then he saw her: a radiant woman clothed with the sun, surrounded by a brilliant light. Speaking tenderly in his native Nahuatl, she called him Juanito, Juan Dieguito, and revealed herself as the Blessed Virgin Mary, Mother of the true God.

She asked him to go to the bishop, Fray Juan de Zumárraga, and request that a church be built on that hill, where she could show her love and compassion to all who sought her Son. Juan obeyed, but the bishop hesitated, asking for a sign to prove the truth of the vision. When Juan returned to Tepeyac, Our Lady promised to provide it.

The next day, Juan did not go to the place where Our Lady had been appearing because his uncle, Juan Bernardino, had fallen gravely ill. Hurrying to find a priest, he tried to avoid the hill, not wanting to delay. Yet Our Lady met him on the path, assuring him, "Am I not here, I who am your Mother?" She told him that his uncle was already healed, and indeed, at that very hour, the man recovered and later confirmed that the Virgin had appeared to him as the *Perfect Virgin, Holy Mary of Guadalupe.*

Then Mary sent Juan to the top of the barren hill to gather the flowers he would find there. In the middle of December, he discovered a garden of Castilian roses. Gathering them in his tilma, he carried them to the bishop. When he opened the cloak, the roses fell—and there, imprinted on the rough fabric, was the image of the Virgin herself. Nearly five centuries later, that miraculous image remains, a living sign that heaven has drawn near.

On the other side of the world, the Catholic Church had lost millions of Catholics to the Protestant reformation. In the Americas, Our Lady responded bringing about the conversion of eight million to the Catholic faith in the seven years that followed the apparitions of Our Lady of Guadalupe.

The Tilma and Miracles

The tilma itself is extraordinary. The image depicts Mary with features reflecting the indigenous people, standing on a crescent moon, adorned with stars, and clothed in a radiant mantle. Scientific study has uncovered numerous remarkable features that defy natural explanation:

- The colors have remained vibrant for nearly 500 years despite exposure to smoke, humidity, and handling. This type of fiber should have only lasted 20 to 30 years.
- Analyses show no evidence of conventional pigments or painting techniques, in fact, we have not found the pigment anywhere else in the world.
- Microscopic studies have revealed that the image has no underlying sketches or brush strokes. The tilma appears to have been created spontaneously in full color and detail.
- Studies have shown that you can see the reflections of Juan Diego and the bishop in the eyes of Our Lady shown with refraction that would have been unknown to the people at the time.
- Infrared and ultraviolet examinations indicate that the fibers of the cactus-cloth are unaffected by known chemical or artistic processes, suggesting the image did not result from human creation.
- Hundreds have testified to have heard two heartbeats coming from the tilma—one louder and slower, and one quieter and faster.

Reflection

Mary's message at Guadalupe extends to us today: She is our Mother. She is not distant or indifferent, but knows us intimately and intercedes for us with the love of a mother. She teaches us to have hope in difficult circumstances while comforting us.

Mary invites us to trust her, to accept her guidance, and to experience the extraordinary ways she manifests God's love in our world. The miraculous tilma, still preserved after nearly five centuries, stands as a tangible reminder that God acts in both the natural and supernatural realms for our salvation and encouragement.

- How do I recognize Mary's maternal presence in my life? How does she comfort, guide, and intercede for me?
- How does knowledge of the tilma's miraculous nature allow me to see Mary's love and tenderness which extends to me in my life?

After the Reflection, pray the Marian Prayers the *Sub Tuum Præsidium,* the *Hail Mary,* and the *Hail Holy Queen.*

Day 13

The Perpetual Virginity of Mary

"How will this be, since I do not know man?"
–Luke 1:34

One of the Church's most unassumingly deep truths about Our Lady is her perpetual virginity—which highlights her holiness, her singular role in salvation history, and God's extraordinary intention in choosing her. This, being the second dogma of Mary, affirms that Mary remained a virgin before, during, and after the birth of Christ. Known as her "threefold virginity," this truth underscores her unique consecration to God and her total participation in the divine plan.

Mary's virginity before the conception of Christ is a well-known truth, and that Mary remained a virgin the rest of her life is also easily accepted by Catholics despite being part of some debates among other Christians. What I have found is the aspect of Mary's virginity most interesting to people is her virginity during the birth of Christ. We will discuss all three aspects of her virginity, and how this beautiful mystery calls us more deeply into a relationship with Our Blessed Mother.

Virgin Before the Birth of Christ

Mary's virginity before the conception and Birth of Christ was foretold well in advance to prepare God's people for His plan of salvation. As we recall the prophesy of Isaiah: "Behold a virgin shall conceive and bear a son" (Is 7:14). This prophesy is then applied directly to the Virgin Mary and Christ by St. Matthew in his Gospel: "All this took place to fulfill what the Lord has spoken by the prophet: Behold, a virgin shall conceive and bear a son" (Mt 1:23) as he described how the Birth of Christ took place.

This virginity before the birth of Christ emphasizes Mary's preparation and total dedication to God's plan. She was consecrated from the very beginning to a life of purity and obedience, marked by grace from the moment of her Immaculate Conception. St. Augustine remarks that Mary was "enclosed within the ark of her own virginity" even before Christ's conception, a vessel prepared to receive the Word of God.

Our Lady's virginity before the Birth of Christ highlights her holiness as a human being untouched by sin, fully open to God's plan. Her purity is not merely physical, but spiritual: it signifies her total surrender and readiness to participate in the mystery of the Incarnation, something we can emulate according to our own state in life.

Virgin During the Birth of Christ

Catholics seem to easily accept that Mary was a virgin before the Birth of Christ and remained a virgin for the duration of her life. But the dogma of Mary's perpetual virginity also emphasizes the miraculous nature of the Birth of Christ. The virginity during the birth—often referred to by the Latin term *virgo partiture*—affirms that Mary gave birth to Jesus without losing her *virginial integrity.*

To understand this, we need to look through the lens of the Jewish ritual cleanness laws and culture. Without going into this in too graphic a nature, the Law stated that even during times of a woman's menstrual cycle she was not considered "clean." A woman was required to wash on certain days and then wait for a period of seven days after the completion of her menstrual phase before going back in to have relations with her husband. Interestingly, this resulted in the married couple having relations frequently near peak fertility, so we see God's plan in having them be fruitful and multiply. As applied to childbirth, the physical birth of a child would also be seen as disturbing a woman's virginal integrity—something from which Mary was entirely preserved to show her great sanctity and the uniqueness of Christ's Birth.

The teaching of the Church is that the Birth of Christ sanctified Mary's virginity rather than harming it (cf. Lumen Gentium, 57). The Fathers' consensus, later explicitly developed, was that Jesus passed through Mary like light passes through a glass—doing no harm to the sacred vessel. Even in the papal definition of Mary's perpetual virginity by Pope Martin I at the First Lateran Council in 649, Mary is said to have maintained her perfect virginity before, *during,* and after the birth of Jesus.

This aspect of her virginity also deepens our understanding of her spiritual purity. Every action of Mary, even the most human, was aligned with God's will, demonstrating perfect holiness. Her cooperation in the miracle of the Incarnation is the model for our own cooperation with grace: every part of our lives, if surrendered to God, can participate in His salvific plan.

Virginity After the Birth of Christ*

Mary's virginity after the birth of Christ shows us the continuity of her holiness, her total consecration to God, and her role as the Ark of the New Covenant. Just as the Ark carried the presence of God through the wilderness, Mary continued to bear the presence of Christ in her life, remaining wholly consecrated and dedicated to Him.

This post-birth virginity also speaks to Mary's perpetual mission as Mother of God and Mother of the Church. It preserves the singularity of her role: she is not merely a vessel at a single moment in time, but a model of holiness and devotion for all generations.

We know that this virginity was intentional, and we hear this directly from Mary's mouth at the Annunciation, as St. Augustine clarifies:

> This is shown by the words which Mary spoke in answer to the Angel announcing to her conception; How, says she, shall this be, seeing I know not a man? Which assuredly she would not say, unless she had before vowed herself unto God as a virgin. (St. Augustine, *De Virginitate*)

Mary's continued virginity points to the specialness of her Son's Birth. No other child could follow from the same sacred vessel as the Godman. Mary's virginity is like every other aspect of her life—it points to Jesus and shows us the honor and devotion we ought to give Him in our own lives.

Reflection

Mary's threefold virginity—before, during, and after birth—reveals the depth of God's intention in salvation history. She was chosen to be the pure vessel of the Incarnation, and her integrity, purity, and obedience made her fit to bear the Son of God. Our devotion to Mary is not merely sentimental; it is rooted in a recognition of this extraordinary holiness.

Mary's virginity is therefore an invitation: to honor her purity, to strive for holiness in our own lives, and to recognize that God can work miracles through those who fully surrender to Him. Her life demonstrates that sanctity is not limited to extraordinary acts; it flows from a total openness to God's will, every day, in every circumstance.

- In what ways do Mary's purity and holiness challenge me to greater surrender to God in my own life?
- How can devotion to Mary inspire me to live a life of obedience, integrity, and cooperation with God's will?

After the Reflection, pray the Marian Prayers the *Sub Tuum Præsidium*, the *Hail Mary*, and the *Hail Holy Queen.*

Supplement

*There are some objections by Protestants on this part of the dogma that would have been too lengthy to include in today's reflection, but I wanted to address them to provide you with adequate responses and a greater understanding of the Church's teaching.

The two main objections by Protestants to Mary's virginity after the Birth of Christ are from Matthew 1:18 and 1:25 and from Mark 6:3 and Matthew 13:55. I would like to answer those **briefly** here.

First Objection:

> "Now the birth of Jesus Christ took place in this way. When his mother Mary had been betrothed to Joseph, *before* they came together she was found to be with child of the Holy Spirit" (Mt. 1:18).

> "When Joseph woke from sleep, he did as the angel of the Lord commanded him; he took his wife, but knew her not *until* she had borne a son" (Mt 1:24–25).

I added emphasis to the words "before" and "until" because these are the words Protestants use to imply that they had relations "after" the mentioned events. The purpose of saying "before" and "until" is not to imply that they had relations after, but to show that Mary did not have any relations beforehand which could have led to a conception. This safeguards the teaching of Jesus' miraculous conception.

Elsewhere in Scripture words like this are used. 2 Samuel 6:23 says, "And Michal the daughter of Saul had no child to the day of her death." Some translations say, "until the day of her death." Well, she certainly did not have any children after the day of her death. The inclusion of "to the day" or "until the day" is meant to say that it did not occur at any point before her death. This is the same intention of Matthew 1:18 and 1:25.

Second Objection:

> "Is not this the carpenter, the son of Mary and brother of James and Joses and Judas and Simons, and are not his sisters here with us?" (Mark 6:3)
>
> "Are not his brethren James and Joseph and Simon and Judas" (Matthew 13:55)

The objection here is that Protestants say that Jesus had biological siblings. The simple answer is that the Greek word for "brother" can mean cousin, near relative, kinsman, etc. Even in the Hebrew, it does not mean biological sibling, because the emphasis was placed on relatives in general. Elizabeth is even called Mary's "kinswoman" although she was likely Mary's aunt.

A good example here is Genesis 13:8 when Lot is called Abraham's "brother" when we know the actual relationship was that of uncle and nephew.

As for those mentioned in regards to Jesus, we know that they had other parents who were not Mary and Joseph.

Day 14

Our Lady of Fatima

"Say the Rosary every day to obtain peace for the world. And after each decade, say the following prayer: 'O my Jesus, forgive us our sins, save us from the fires of Hell, lead all souls to Heaven, especially those in most need of Thy mercy.'"

–Our Lady of Fatima

The apparitions of Our Lady of Fatima are perhaps the most well-known apparitions besides Our Lady of Guadalupe. She came as the powerful "Lady of the Rosary" to remind us that her role in salvation history is not confined to Scripture or the Early Church, but that it continues today. God desires to establish a devotion to her and her Immaculate Heart, through which souls are guided toward Christ. Fatima is a clear continuation of the mission of Christ, where Mary and the Holy Spirit work in union to bring the world closer to God.

The Apparitions

In 1917, during the turmoil of World War I, Mary appeared six times to three shepherd children—Lucia, Francisco, and Jacinta—in the small village of Fatima, Portugal. The world was in chaos, the faithful were struggling, and the Church faced both internal and external challenges. Into this moment, Mary intervened not with condemnation, but with maternal guidance, prophecy, and a call to holiness.

Calling herself the Lady of the Rosary, she asked the children to pray the Rosary daily, to make sacrifices for sinners, and to spread devotion to her Immaculate Heart. Her simple message stated: through Mary, God desires to bring souls to His Son, to deepen their prayer life, and to foster holiness in the midst of worldly trials.

Our Lady stressed the urgency of these prayers, foretelling that if the world did not turn away from sin and toward God in prayer, there would be an even greater war than Europe had just experienced. She prophesied that the war to come would be preceded by a night illumined by an unknown light, and in 1938, a widespread aurora borealis lit up the night sky all across Europe. World War II began shortly after.

One of the signs that Our Lady famously gave was the *Miracle of the Sun*. Our Lady had promised to perform miracles on October 13, 1917, and in response 70,000 people showed up to watch. After months of skepticism and ridicule, the crowd stood under a pouring rain when suddenly the clouds broke, and the sun appeared as a spinning disc of light. It pulsed with brilliant colors, whirled across the sky, and seemed to plunge toward the earth—causing fear and awe among the onlookers. Then, just as suddenly, it returned to its place, and everyone's soaked clothes and the muddy ground were instantly dry.

Among the witnesses were two Freemasons who had come as journalists, intending to mock and discredit the events.

They were not believers and had planned to publish an article exposing the "superstition" of the crowds. But when they saw the phenomenon with their own eyes, they were shaken. Instead of the attack piece they meant to write, they described the miracle as it happened—truthfully and without ridicule—testifying to what they had seen along with thousands of others.

The Messages of Fatima

The messages of Fatima are deeply Christ-centered. Mary repeatedly emphasizes the need for conversion, prayer, and penance:

- Prayer: The Rosary, as Mary instructed, is a tool for meditation on Christ's life, death, and resurrection. Through repeated prayer, the faithful are drawn into the mysteries of salvation.
- Sacrifice and penance: The children were called to offer small acts of reparation for the sins of the world. This echoes the Gospel teaching that suffering united to Christ can bring grace and holiness.
- Devotion to the Immaculate Heart: Mary revealed that her Heart is a channel through which God pours grace into the world. By consecrating ourselves to her Immaculate Heart, we cooperate with God's work and grow closer to Christ.

Mary's messages at Fatima consistently point to one truth: God desires to save souls, and He chooses to do so through Mary's maternal guidance and mediation. The Holy Spirit works in harmony with her, confirming her words with signs and miracles, drawing hearts to Christ.

> Sacrifice yourselves for sinners, and say often, especially when making some sacrifice: 'O Jesus, this is for love of You, for the conversion of sinners, and in reparation for the sins committed against the Immaculate Heart of Mary.' (Our Lady to the Children of Fatima)

The Five First Saturdays

Our Lady also asked the children to honor her in a special way for five consecutive first Saturdays of the month in a row and thus asked of us to honor the devotion of the Five First Saturdays. In this devotion, she requested that the faithful go to Confession, receive Holy Communion, pray five decades of the Rosary, and spend fifteen minutes meditating on its mysteries—all with the intention of making reparation to her Immaculate Heart.

Each of the five Saturdays corresponds to a particular offense against Our Lady: against her Immaculate Conception, her perpetual virginity, her divine maternity, the rejection of her as Mother of all humanity, and the desecration of her sacred images. Through this devotion, we console her heart wounded by ingratitude and blasphemy, and we unite ourselves more deeply to the Heart of her Son, answering her call at Fatima for prayer, repentance, and the conversion of the world.

Those who faithfully honor this devotion, fulfilling all that Our Lady requested with love and reparation, are promised the graces necessary for salvation at the hour of death. The Blessed Virgin herself assured that she will be present with the mercy of her Son in their final moments, bringing peace and the help needed to persevere in grace. She also promised that this devotion would bring about the salvation of many sinners and peace in the world.

Reflection

Mary calls us to holiness, to prayer, and to reparation, always pointing toward Christ. The messages and miracles demonstrate that God works in both extraordinary and ordinary ways, and that the cooperation of the faithful—like the children of Fatima—is essential in responding to His plan.

- In what ways can I deepen my prayer life, especially through the Rosary, as a response to Our Lady's call?
- How can I participate in the mission of bringing souls closer to Christ, as Mary and the Spirit invite us to do?

After the Reflection, pray the Marian Prayers the *Sub Tuum Præsidium*, the *Hail Mary*, and the *Hail Holy Queen.*

Day 15

The Immaculate Conception

> *"The Most Blessed Virgin Mary was, from the first moment of her conception, by a singular grace and privilege of Almighty God, in view of the merits of Jesus Christ, Savior of the human race, preserved immune from all stain of original sin."*
>
> *–Pope Pius IX, Ineffabilis Deus, 1854*

The Immaculate Conception is perhaps the most misrepresented of the four Marian dogmas because popular culture—television, movies, books, etc.—often refer to the miraculous conception of Jesus as the "Immaculate Conception." In reality, the Immaculate Conception speaks not of the conception of Jesus, but rather describes the natural conception of Mary by her two parents Sts. Joachim and Anne. Although I say the word "natural" I do not want you to think that there is nothing supernatural in this. Mary was conceived by natural means, but this dogma teaches that Mary was preserved from all stain of Original Sin from the very first moment of her existence. Unlike the rest of humanity, who inherit the effects of sin, Mary was granted a singular grace, preparing her to be the pure dwelling place for the Son of God.

The Holy Ark of the New Covenant

Mary's Immaculate Conception was a fitting way to prepare His people for the coming of the Messiah, when God Himself would take on human flesh. Just as the Ark of the Covenant was called holy (cf. 2 Chronicles 35:3), Mary was made holy from the first moment of her existence so she would be the fitting dwelling place of the Son of God for nine months while He was in her womb, taking His human nature from her and being nourished by her.

We recall the beautiful words spoken to Mary at the Annunciation by the Angel Gabriel, "Hail, full of grace" (Luke 1:28), a greeting so mysterious that had even Mary perplexed at what sort of greeting it was. This is because the word the angel used was never before used to speak of a person; it is the Greek *kecharitomene,* which doesn't simply mean "highly favored" as some translations render it. The reason this word had such a dramatic effect on Our Lady is because the tense the word is in. Grammatically *kecharitomene* is a perfect passive participle—so for those of you who are not linguists, this means that the word denotes that the one to whom the message is spoken (Mary from the angel) is the recipient of an action in whom the action has already been completed.

Simplified, this means that the angel is saying Mary has already been filled with grace. The action has already taken place in its fullness; she has already been perfectly filled with grace. Now you can see how this has big implications for Mary's role in salvation and in our understanding of who she is.

A Man, a Woman, and A Tree

Unfortunately, we live in a time where many non-Catholic Christians have tried to downplay Mary's role in salvation history, even denying her Immaculate Conception. But if we take a few steps back, it simply makes sense that God would prepare a dwelling place for Himself, and that He would honor the Fourth Commandment by blessing His own Mother through His work of salvation.

The Immaculata, the Mother of God, is the one whom God prepared not only to be His vessel, but to be the be the Woman who would participate in bringing the redemption to the world. In the beginning God charged Adam with protecting the Garden of Eden and his wife, Eve. He was the first priest. Oftentimes we hear Original Sin reduced to the sin of Eve who took an apple, but truly the Original Sin was that Adam did not fulfill his priestly obligations by protecting his wife from the serpent, who made his way into the garden. Then Eve was tempted by that serpent and ate of the fruit of the Tree of Knowledge of Good and Evil and gave some to her husband. In short, Original Sin was committed by a man with the active participation of a woman.

So too, God's plan was to bring about salvation by a perfect man (God Himself made flesh) with the participation of a woman (the Woman first prophesied in Genesis 3:15, who would become the Woman at the Wedding at Cana, at the Cross, and in Revelation): Mary. This plan also involves a tree: the new Tree of Life, the Cross.

Enmity—Total, Radical Opposition

Immediately after the Fall, God told the serpent that He would put enmity between the Woman to come and the serpent (cf. Genesis 3:15). This word enmity means a complete, total, and radical opposition. This means that the Woman who would bear the Savior would be completely at odds with the Devil. Mary would not have true enmity with the Devil if she had any sin or concupiscence. Instead, God prepared her to be the one who would crush his head. God is the one who sits opposite to sin—since sin is the rejection of God and His Law—and Mary sits opposite the Devil—she is the perfect creature, while the Devil is the most fallen creature.

How Mary was Redeemed

It is also necessary, I think, to address the main obstacle to defining this dogma. People love to say that St. Thomas Aquinas, the Angelic Doctor of the Church, denied the Immaculate Conception. This is not really an honest statement. St. Thomas believed that Mary was sinless in her life and was purified immediately after conception. His issue was that he could not figure out how Jesus would be the Universal Redeemer if He did not also redeem Mary. He held that the merits of Christ were applied to Mary as soon as she was conceived, but not instantaneously.

The answer came with Blessed John Duns Scotus, who explained that Mary was saved by God through what he called "Preventative Redemption." To use an analogy, this is like if someone was about to get hit by a car and another person ran into the street and pulled them away before the car hit them. We would rightly say that the hero saved the person from getting hit, just as we would say someone who rushed the person to the hospital after getting hit saved them.

God saved Mary by preserving her from all stain of Original Sin. The merits from the Cross were applied to Mary at the moment of her conception, further emphasizing Christ as

Universal Redeemer. This is the stance the Church has taken, which was then solemnly defined on December 8, 1854 by Pope Pius IX.

Reflection

From the graces of the Immaculate Conception, Mary's holiness surpasses that of all the angels and saints. Her perfection is a singular privilege, but meant as a gift to all of us. Her Immaculate Conception was given in view of Mary's vocation to be the Mother of God, and also for her vocation as Mother of the Church.

- How does understanding Mary's Immaculate Conception strengthen my trust in her role as my spiritual Mother?
- In what ways can I imitate Mary's openness to God's will in my daily choices and actions?

After the Reflection, pray the Marian Prayers the *Sub Tuum Præsidium*, the *Hail Mary*, and the *Hail Holy Queen.*

Day 16

Our Lady of Lourdes: "I am the Immaculate Conception"

"I am the Immaculate Conception."
– Our Lady to St. Bernadette Soubirous,
February 11, 1858

In 1854, when Pope Pius IX stepped out on the balcony to proclaim the dogma of Mary's Immaculate Conception, the stormy skies were cloudy and the day was dreary. When he began to speak the words of proclamation, "We declare, pronounce, and define..." the clouds opened up, and a ray of sunlight shone down directly upon the Pope. This was seen as a divine confirmation that God and the Immaculata were pleased with this definition. Only four years after this dogmatic definition did Our Lady give another confirmation of her Immaculate Conception in the apparitions of Our Lady of Lourdes.

In the small village of Lourdes, France, Mary appeared to a poor, uneducated girl named Bernadette Soubirous, and her words carried profound theological significance. When St.

Bernadette asked the Lady her name, she replied, *"I am the Immaculate Conception."* In doing so, Mary confirmed the Church's teaching in a personal and intimate way, revealing herself to the world as the one preserved from all sin by a singular grace of God. Not only did Mary speak the truth of the Immaculate Conception, but she stated it as her name, indicating that the Immaculate Conception speaks to us of Mary's very identity.

The Apparitions

In 1858, the fourteen-year-old Bernadette reported seeing a beautiful Lady in a grotto near the Gave River in France. The Lady spoke with humility and gentleness, instructing Bernadette to pray and do penance. Initially, Mary's exclamation—*"I am the Immaculate Conception"*—was met with skepticism by the local clergy and bishop, because Bernadette herself did not know what it meant and she was not well educated. Mary, however, revealed this truth to her in a way that underscored both her holiness and the teaching of the Church. St. Bernadette's lack of theological education actually became key evidence showing that these apparitions were legitimate, because she could not have known this truth otherwise.

By identifying herself in this manner, Mary affirmed her sinless state and reminded all who heard her of the immense grace given to her in preparation for her role as Mother of God. She also began to reveal something essential about who she is. She is the Immaculate Conception—she is the one perfectly united to the Holy Spirit from the moment of her conception. It is the overshadowing of the Spirit that made this new Ark of the Covenant truly holy. The Church understands that Mary has a unique relationship with the Holy Spirit as a living temple of

His presence. And as we shall discuss in the reflection on St. Maximilian Kolbe's Mariology next, we see that Mary lives in a profound union with the Holy Spirit.

The Message of Lourdes

The message of Lourdes is consistent with all Marian apparitions throughout history: Mary always calls us to her Son, adapting the same message to the needs of different times and places. Mary's words and actions at Lourdes call the faithful to three essential time-tested practices:

1. **Pray from the heart:** Mary repeatedly instructed Bernadette to pray for sinners, emphasizing personal devotion and sincere petition. True prayer, she teaches, is not merely recited words, but heartfelt communication with God through her intercession.
2. **Repent and frequent the Sacraments:** Mary calls the faithful to conversion. Sin disrupts our relationship with God, but through repentance and the regular reception of the Sacraments, we can receive forgiveness and grow in true holiness.
3. **Pray the Rosary:** The Rosary is central to Mary's apparitions because it draws us into the mysteries of Christ's life, Death, and Resurrection. At Lourdes, she invited not only Bernadette but all who would listen to unite daily prayer with acts of sacrifice, fostering deeper communion with her Son. The Rosary is the weapon that defeats evil and a most powerful tool by which we enter into the mysteries of the lives of Jesus and Mary.

The Miraculous Spring

Perhaps the most famous aspect of Lourdes is the healing spring that Mary revealed to Bernadette. Our Lady told Bernadette to "drink from the spring and wash," yet there was no spring to be seen. Obediently, Bernadette knelt down and began to dig in the dirt with her hands, uncovering only a small pool of muddy water.

To those watching, her actions seemed odd and confusing—but before long, clear water began to flow from the ground, growing into a spring that still runs today. This miraculous water became a sign of healing and purification, drawing countless pilgrims to Lourdes from around the world.

Water from the grotto has been associated with thousands of miraculous healings, recognized by the Church after rigorous investigation. These healings are not just physical but often carry spiritual significance: the sick are drawn into prayer, their faith is strengthened, and many experience conversion of heart.

Reflection

Mary's message at Lourdes reveals a consistent pattern in Marian apparitions. They are always Christocentric: she leads us to prayer, encourages repentance, and calls us to embrace God's grace in our daily lives. The healing waters, the call to holiness, and her maternal presence all point toward the same goal—bringing souls closer to Christ.

We also see that Mary's Immaculate Conception unites her to the mission of the Holy Spirit. When Christ ascended, He and the Father sent the Holy Spirit. Mary, too, was present at Pentecost, and already filled with the Spirit she interceded for the Church. Today she continues working with the Spirit, going out in the world to bring the bound and broken to her Son.

- In what ways can I participate in Mary's invitation to pray, repent, and frequent the Sacraments?
- How do the miraculous healings at Lourdes remind me of God's active presence in the world today?

After the Reflection, pray the Marian Prayers the *Sub Tuum Præsidium*, the *Hail Mary*, and the *Hail Holy Queen*.

Day 17

St. Maximilian Kolbe and the Immaculata

"The Holy Spirit is far too little known."
–St. Maximilian Kolbe

When St. Bernadette asked the Lady at Lourdes her name, Mary responded with a phrase that greatly perplexed St. Maximilian Kolbe. He points out that Mary did not say, "I was conceived without sin," but rather, "I am the Immaculate Conception." He further explains that this reveals not only what happened to Mary, but who she is. Her very identity is the Immaculate Conception itself—immaculateness personified in human form.

Just as God revealed His name to Moses, saying, "I AM WHO AM," expressing that He is existence itself, Mary's revelation to Bernadette expresses that she is the created reflection of that divine reality. She is the Immaculate Conception—the one conceived in time, yet totally belonging to God from the first instant of her existence.

This led Kolbe to his frequent question, "Who then are you O Immaculate?" This is a question I often ponder, too. As such, I have spent a lot of time with Kolbe's writings. As a result, this reflection is a little longer and more theological, but please bear with me. This is something you won't want to miss! This is a window into the mystery of Mary and the Holy Spirit which has huge implications for your everyday prayer life and mine.

The Spirit and the Immaculata

The answer to Kolbe's question came in a meditation on the Person of the Holy Spirit. St. Maximilian came to the conclusion that the Holy Spirit is the Uncreated Immaculate Conception. The Father eternally begets the Son; the Son is eternally begotten of the Father; and the Holy Spirit is the eternal, uncreated fruit of the love between the Father and the Son.

> Who is the Spirit? He is the fruit of the love of the Father and the Son. The fruit of created love is a created conception. The Spirit, therefore, is an uncreated eternal conception. . . .The Spirit, therefore, is a most holy conception, infinitely holy, immaculate.[4]

The Spirit, then, is the uncreated Immaculate Conception—pure, holy love—"the flowering of the love between the Father and the Son."

---

[4] Maximilian Kolbe, "1318 Immaculate Conception," in *The Writings of St. Maximilian Maria Kolbe*, vol. 2, *Various Writings* (Lugano, Italy: Nerbini International, 2016), 2301.

Kolbe saw that Mary mirrors this reality perfectly. The Holy Spirit is the uncreated Immaculate Conception; Mary is the created Immaculate Conception. It was the Spirit's action that formed her immaculate heart in her mother's womb, and it was again His overshadowing that made her the Mother of God. Mary's Immaculate Conception, therefore, is both the work and the revelation of the Holy Spirit.

This is why the angel greets her in Luke 1:28 not by name, but by title: "Hail, full of grace." As we recall, the Greek word, *kecharitomene,* means "you who have been perfected by grace." It is a perfect passive participle—indicating that this perfection was already complete in her. No one else in Scripture is ever greeted this way. The angel does not merely describe Mary's state of grace; he identifies her by it. This is her very name.

Mary, the Created Immaculate Conception

Kolbe understood that at the moment of Mary's conception, the Holy Spirit poured into her a superabundance of grace—greater than that of all angels and saints combined. She was made entirely pure, entirely united to God. The Spirit, the "fount of all holiness," gave her His own name, Immaculate Conception.

Kolbe compared this to marriage:

> If, among the creatures, a bride receives the groom's name, because she belongs to him and joins him, is made similar to him and, in union with him, becomes the creative agent of life, all the more so, the name of the Holy Spirit, "Immaculate Conception" is the name of the

> One in whom He lives with a love that is fruitful throughout the whole supernatural order.[5]

Yet even this analogy falls short, because Mary's union with the Spirit surpasses any human intimacy. He lives and acts in her in a way beyond our comprehension. Kolbe writes, "The Third Person of the Blessed Trinity never took flesh; still, our human word 'spouse' is far too weak to express the reality of the relationship between the Immaculata and the Holy Spirit."

Mary is not the incarnation of the Holy Spirit—the Spirit never became flesh—but her union with Him is so perfect that Kolbe called her the *quasi-incarnatus,* the "quasi-incarnate" of the Holy Spirit. Every thought, word, and action of Mary was imbued with the presence and power of the Spirit. In her, the Holy Spirit makes Himself visible and approachable to the world.

Just as the divine and human natures of Christ are united without mixture or division in one Divine Person, Kolbe saw that Mary and the Holy Spirit are united so intimately—while remaining two distinct persons—that they "live one sole life." Wherever Mary is, there the Spirit is also. Wherever the Spirit acts, He acts through her.

The Mission of the Spirit Through Mary

This union is not one-sided. Just as every act of Mary is filled with the Spirit, Mary is united to the Holy Spirit as He acts in the world today. Kolbe wrote, "The Holy Spirit only works

---

[5] Maximilian Kolbe, "1318 Immaculate Conception."

through the Immaculata, His Bride. Accordingly, she is the Mediatrix of all graces of the Holy Spirit."[6]

Every grace we receive from God—every movement of conversion, every inspiration of charity—comes to us from Christ through the Holy Spirit, and Mary is united to the Spirit interceding for us. This is why she is called "full of grace," and why the Church rightly calls her Mediatrix.

Wherever we find Mary, we find the living action of the Holy Spirit. And wherever the Spirit moves, His Spouse is present with Him. This is profoundly consoling: when we approach Mary in prayer, we can be absolutely sure that the Holy Spirit Himself is present in that prayer. Her intercession is never empty, for it is entirely united to His divine will.

Kolbe and many saints after him have said that Mary's intercession is "omnipotent"—not by nature, but by grace. God alone is all-powerful, yet Mary's prayers, perfectly united to the Spirit, are always heard. She asks only what God wills, and thus she obtains everything she asks. Through her, grace flows from the Father, through the Son, in the Spirit—to us. And through her, our prayers ascend again to the Father, through the same divine order.

Reflection

The mission of the Holy Spirit—and therefore of Mary—is to bring souls into communion with God. The Spirit transforms us from within, making us sons and daughters of the Father in the Son. Mary, the Mediatrix and Spouse of the Spirit, participates in this same mission, leading us to her Son

[6] Maximilian Kolbe, "634 To Br. Salezy Mikołajczyk, Niepokalanów," in *The Writings of St. Maximilian Maria Kolbe*, vol. 1, *Letters* (Lugano, Italy: Nerbini International, 2016), 1178.

with the simple words she spoke at Cana: "Do whatever He tells you" (John 2:5).

Through her, Christ entered the world; through her, He continues to come to souls today. Kolbe knew that it is only through her, the one through whom the Spirit works, that the head of the serpent can be crushed.

If we give ourselves entirely to Mary, she will make us instruments of the Holy Spirit—spiritual warriors in her army of grace. For where the Immaculata is, there too is the power of God Himself.

- How do I understand Mary as the Mediatrix of all graces of the Holy Spirit? How can this inspire more confidence in the prayers I ask of her?
- Set aside some time to ask Mary to reveal to you the presence of the Holy Spirit. Sit in silence in His presence.

After the Reflection, pray the Marian Prayers the *Sub Tuum Præsidium*, the *Hail Mary*, and the

Day 18

The Assumption of Mary

"We pronounce, declare, and define it to be a divinely revealed dogma: that the Immaculate Mother of God, the ever Virgin Mary, having completed the course of her earthly life, was assumed body and soul into heavenly glory."

– Pope Pius XII, Munificentissimus Deus, 1950

The fourth and most recent Marian dogma to be defined by the Church is the Assumption. This does not mean that the Church did not believe this truth in the Early Church, but that, through the development of doctrine, this was solemnly defined most recently. All dogmas of the faith have been believed at least implicitly since the beginning of the Church.

The dogma of the Assumption of Mary states: at the end of her earthly life, Mary was taken, body and soul, into heaven. This extraordinary privilege demonstrates her holiness and points to the destiny God offers to all the faithful in the resurrection of the dead. Mary's Assumption is also about discipleship. Her life, death, and glorification reveal the path of faithful obedience that God desires for each of us.

The Ark of the Covenant Taken to Heaven

Mary's Assumption highlights her unique perfection. Unlike all other humans, her body was preserved from corruption, retaining the gifts God had bestowed upon Adam and Eve before the Fall. In Genesis 3:15, Mary's enmity with the serpent foreshadows her participation with her Son in the total victory over the Devil and sin. Pope Pius XII, in defining this dogma, reflects upon these realities from Genesis. He states that the effects of sin include death, at least death by material corruption. He then concludes that Mary triumphs over both sin and death. She triumphs over sin by her Immaculate Conception, and she triumphs over death by her glorious Assumption. The Assumption is the fitting effect of the Immaculate Conception.

We recall that Mary as the Ark of the New Covenant is holy—and the resurgence of the Ark is seen in the book of Revelation, when John describes seeing the Ark in Heaven and then immediately describes the Woman clothed with the sun, with the moon beneath her feet, and a crown of twelve stars. As such, the Church celebrates the Coronation of Mary as Queen of Heaven and Earth on the Octave (8th day following) the Solemnity of the Assumption of Mary, body and soul, into heavenly glory.

The Dormition

The Assumption also reveals the intimate connection between grace and discipleship. Mary's entire life was oriented toward God: her *fiat* at the Annunciation, her journey to Elizabeth, her intercession at Cana, and her standing beneath the Cross. Each act prepared her for the glory that awaited her. Mary's Assumption is the visible fruit of a life conformed to God's will.

Mary's perfect discipleship explains many in the Early Church, particularly in the East held about Mary's Assumption, calling it the *Dormition of Mary,* or Mary's "falling asleep." The Eastern tradition, still celebrated by the Eastern Orthodox and Eastern Catholic Churches, states that at the end of Mary's earthly life, she had a separation of her body and soul (death) for three days. During this time Mary descended to the souls in Purgatory, consoling them in imitation of her Son who descended to the dead after His Crucifixion (cf. 1 Peter 3:19). Just as Christ remained with the dead until the third day, this tradition holds that Mary remained offering comfort, until on the third day she was taken up body and soul into heaven.

In the Church in the West, the language of the definition of the Assumption is left slightly ambiguous. By this I mean the Church has not specifically stated whether or not Mary died. One thing is clear, though, if Mary did die, it was not due to bodily corruption. Instead it would have been done out of perfect discipleship and conformity to her Son. As Catholics, we may hold either opinion so long as we acknowledge her lack of corruption. And, although the West has not spoken definitively on this matter, Pope St. John Paul II did mention Mary's death in a Wednesday audience. Additionally, it is a tradition of the devotion to the Brown Scapular that Mary comforts the souls in Purgatory each Saturday—an implicit affirmation of the tradition of the Dormition.

Mary's Mediation

The traditions of the Assumption and Dormition of Mary both remind us of her continued mission to mediate the presence of God to humanity. In the Dormition we see her bringing comfort to the souls in Purgatory through her presence and intercession. In the Assumption itself we see Mary taken up into heavenly glory, where the Church says:

> Taken up to heaven she did not lay aside this salvific duty, but by her constant intercession continued to bring us the gifts of eternal salvation. By her maternal charity, she cares for the brethren of her Son, who still journey on earth surrounded by dangers and cultics, until they are led into the happiness of their true home. Therefore the Blessed Virgin is invoked by the Church under the titles of Advocate, Auxiliatrix, Adjutrix, and Mediatrix. This, however, is to be so understood that it neither takes away from nor adds anything to the dignity and efficaciousness of Christ the one Mediator. –*Lumen Gentium*, 62

Reflection

I, for one, am comforted by the thought of the Dormition of Mary, because it emphasizes what it means to be a true disciple of Christ, who was "obedient unto death, and death on a cross" (Philippians 2:8). Mary shows us what it truly means to follow her Son's exhortation to, "deny himself, take up his cross, and follow me" (Matthew 16:24). Her glorious Assumption reminds us of her constant work in continuing the mission of her Son in caring for us, her spiritual children.

- How does Mary's descent to the souls in Purgatory inspire me to pray for those who have died?

- How can I deny myself in some small way today, and choose to follow Christ more closely in imitation of Mary?

After the Reflection, pray the Marian Prayers the *Sub Tuum Præsidium*, the *Hail Mary*, and the *Hail Holy Queen*.

Day 19

The Coronation of Mary

"Oh! When will the time come when you, O Queen of heaven, become Queen of ***all people*** *and of* ***each person individually****? With your help, within the limits of our ability, we shall fight for that goal to our last breath. Help us, then, O Queen, Lady, Most Loving Mother!"*

–St. Maximilian Kolbe

"May the time come as soon as possible in which we can say: THE IMMACULATA IS THE QUEEN OF ALL AND OF EVERY SINGLE PERSON."

–St. Maximilian Kolbe

We have already spoken of the Immaculata as the Queen of Heaven and Earth, but following our reflection on the Assumption of Mary, it is fitting to treat her coronation and how we might crown her in our own spiritual lives. The Church celebrates the Coronation of Mary as Queen of Heaven and Earth (August 22) on the octave of the Solemnity of the Assumption (August 15). An octave is the culmination of the celebration of an event—it is meant to add emphasis to that event and be, pun intended, the crowning jewel. Just as the octave of Easter celebrates God's Divine Mercy (which is given to us through the Passion, Death, and Resurrection of Christ), so the Coronation of Mary shows us that her Assumption was not just Mary's early access to heaven, but her taking her rightful seat in the Kingdom of Heaven—at the right hand of her Son.

This mystery naturally follows the Assumption, for divine love always moves from grace to glory, from humility to exaltation. The Son who once received His humanity from her now shares His heavenly majesty with her. Mary's glorification does not end with being taken up into heaven—it reaches its climax when she is enthroned beside her Son, crowned with the crown of twelve stars.

We can imagine the celebration in heaven when the Blessed Virgin was crowned, taking her place in the seat of the Queen Mother. All of heaven—angels and saints—rejoiced; angels because the Queen of Angels, Queen of Apostles, Queen of Patriarchs, Queen of Martyrs, and Queen of all Saints was crowned in heavenly glory.

It is a personal opinion of mine that this feast is often overlooked. In general, we as Catholics do not celebrate the liturgical calendar outside of church as much as we should. Unfortunately, much of our "at home" celebration revolves around Christmas and Easter. We decorate our homes, put up a tree, listen to Advent and Christmas music, color some eggs, and have Easter baskets for children, but have lost so many beautiful traditions more closely associated with the practice of our faith. In truly following the liturgical calendar, the Assumption of Mary would begin a week-long celebration that we ought to take from the celebration of the Mass into our personal prayer lives, and into our homes. Celebrate with your families all week long, and when the octave comes, crown Mary as the Queen of your families and your homes.

The Devotion Owed to Mary

Catholics make careful distinctions in the honor and devotion we give to God, to the Blessed Virgin Mary, to St. Joseph, and to the saints. You may have heard from non-Catholics that Catholics "worship" Mary and the saints, and then you hear the quick Catholic response of, "No! We venerate them!" So I want to break this down a little for you. The word "worship" as we use it today has been narrowed down to that which we only owe to God. Historically the word "worship" was used more broadly to include a few different things. I say this up front in case you encounter people doing historical research and conflating terms.

Worship traditionally included both the Latin *latria* (which we refer to as adoration)—which belongs to God alone, and the Latin *dulia* (which we refer to as veneration)—this is the honor we give the saints. Today when the word "worship" is used, people are primarily only referring to adoration due to God alone.

To offer adoration to any creature would be idolatry. Yet, because God's grace truly transforms His saints and makes them sharers in His glory, the Church rightly gives them honor and veneration, not as rivals to God but as signs of His power at work in them. We also rightly ask their intercession as we are one Body, the Church, with them.

Mary, however, stands in a class entirely her own. As the Mother of God, the Immaculate Conception, and the Queen of Heaven, she is owed a higher form of veneration called *hyperdulia*—different in both quality and quantity (that is, we give her more honor and a unique honor from other saints).

This honor surpasses that given to any other creature because of her singular grace and intimate cooperation in the mystery of our salvation. St. Joseph, her most chaste spouse and the earthly father of Jesus, is likewise given special honor—greater than that of all the other saints, though less than Mary—called *protodulia* (*proto* meaning "first"). He is the first among the saints after Our Lady, the model of hidden virtue and faithful guardianship. Thus, the order of honor is clear: *latria* to God alone, *hyperdulia* to the Blessed Virgin, *protodulia* to St. Joseph, and *dulia* to all the saints who reflect the light of divine glory.

Reflection

True Marian consecration is the crowning jewel of Marian devotion. It fulfills Mary's Queenship, allowing her to exercise her maternal mediation most fully in us. When we entrust ourselves entirely to her, she takes possession of our hearts—not to rule apart from Christ, but to lead us wholly to Him. Her reign within us ensures that Christ reigns within us. As St. Louis de Montfort teaches, "He, the Holy Ghost, the more He finds Mary, His dear and indissoluble Spouse, in any soul, becomes the more active and mighty in producing Jesus Christ in that soul, and that soul in Jesus Christ."

Every Hail Mary we pray is another jewel in the crown we place upon her head in our spiritual lives. This is why the most powerful Marian prayer, the Rosary, which we will discuss more in a later reflection, is called the "Corona," the "Crown" of Mary. We crown her when we pray the Rosary, and thus live our Marian consecration more perfectly.

- How can I crown Mary more in my personal prayer life and within my family's life at home?

- Take some time to pray the Rosary today. Meditate especially on the decades of the Assumption and the Coronation of Mary.

After the Reflection, pray the Marian Prayers the *Sub Tuum Præsidium*, the *Hail Mary*, and the *Hail Holy Queen.*

Day 20

Mary's Mediation and Role in Salvation

"The poison to deceive man was presented to him by a woman; through a woman salvation for man's recovery is presented."

—St. Augustine

From the moment of her Immaculate Conception, Mary was uniquely prepared by God to be the Woman foretold in Genesis 3:15, the Woman at enmity with the serpent, who, with her seed, would crush the head of the serpent. Her *fiat* at the Annunciation was not a passive consent but an active participation in the divine plan of salvation. In her, God's Word took flesh; through her, the Redeemer entered the world. The mystery of Redemption, then, did not begin on Calvary, but in Nazareth—when the Virgin freely cooperated with God's will, allowing the eternal Word to assume our humanity within her womb.

As we have spoken of before, the Fall came about from the sin of one man with the participation of a woman. God, in his fittingness, chose to bring about our salvation through the redeeming action of the God-Man with the participation of a Woman. It is quite simple, really, as St. Teresa of Calcutta put it, "Without Mary, there is no Jesus."

Mary's Participation in Our Redemption

Mary's role was not simply to become a vessel for the Word Incarnate and then go on her merry way, yet unfortunately this is how many non-Catholics see Our Lady. What they aren't often willing to confront is that they have, in effect, made Mary out to be a surrogate mother. There is nothing further from the truth! Mary's role in our redemption continues far beyond her *fiat*, beyond her raising Christ quietly in her home. It extends not only to the foot of the Cross and the Upper Room and Pentecost, but continues even today.

Mary's participation in our redemption does not imply that she adds anything to the infinite Sacrifice of Christ, but recognizes her unique and subordinate participation in the saving work accomplished by her Son. It acknowledges that God in His infinite wisdom, deigned to come to us through a Woman who would have an active participatory role alongside her Son as the Mother of all the faithful in the order of grace.

All of us participate in our own redemption and the redemption of others through our prayers and sacrifices united to Christ's, yet Mary does so in a singular and unique way, participating even in Christ's Passion itself, standing by His side and offering her suffering to His. It is in this context that Christ gave her to us as Mother when he said the words to the Beloved Disciple, "Behold your mother" (John 19:27).

The prophecy of Simeon foretold of this, when she was told that "a sword would pierce through your own soul also, that the thoughts out of many hearts shall be revealed" (Luke 2:35). St. Alphonsus Ligouri says of this:

> Thus also did Mary suffer all those torments, scourges, thorns, nails, and the cross, which tortured the innocent flesh of Jesus, all entered at the same time into the heart of this Blessed Virgin, to complete her martyrdom. "He suffered in "the flesh, and she in her heart," writes that Blessed Amadeus. "So much so," says Saint Lawrence Justinian, "that the heart of Mary became, as it were, a mirror of the Passion of the Son, in which might be seen, faithfully reflected, the spitting, the blows and wounds, and all that Jesus suffered." Saint Bonaventure also remarks that "those wounds—which were scattered over the body of our Lord were all united in the single heart of Mary."[7]

Mary's Role Continued Today

It is precisely because of this intimate union with Christ in His redeeming work that Mary becomes Mediatrix. Having participated with the Redeemer in His obtaining of the graces of salvation, she is now entrusted by Him to intercede for our needs and assist us with our receptivity to these graces. Just as Eve's cooperation with Adam brought death into the world, Mary's cooperation with the New Adam brings life. All grace flows from Christ, the one Mediator between God and man—but Christ Himself came to us through the channel God has

---

[7] St. Alphonsus Liguori, *The Glories of Mary*, excerpt "Of the Dolours of Mary," on EWTN, https://www.ewtn.com/catholicism/library/of-the-dolours-of-mary-5159

chosen: the Immaculata, who continues her role of mediating the gifts of God to us today. As St. Bernardine of Siena said which was quoted by Pope Leo XIII in his encyclical *Iucunda Sempter Expectatione,* "Every grace that is communicated to this world has a threefold course. For by excellent order, it is dispensed from God to Christ, from Christ to the Virgin, from the Virgin to us."

Our Lady's mediation is both universal and maternal. It is universal because she intercedes for all of humanity to come to know and love her Son, and to receive the graces of salvation He merited on the Cross. It is maternal because her role is not that of a distant administrator, but of a Mother who truly cares for her children and their needs.

Additionally, Mary's union with the Holy Spirit as His indissoluble Spouse shows her union to Him in the work of dispensing of the "gifts which Jesus gained for us by His Death" (St. Pius X, *Ad Diem Illum*). St. Paul, in his Letter to the Corinthians, says the distribution of graces depends on the will of the Holy Spirit (cf. 1 Corinthians 12:8–11), and as we will discuss in two of our upcoming reflections, Mary is intimately united to the Spirit in this task. Everything the Holy Spirit does, Mary is there united to Him, and everything Mary does, she does in perfect union with the Holy Spirit who dwells within her.

Reflection

Our sufferings have meaning. All of our sufferings and sacrifices can be united to Christ's on the Cross as an offering which benefits us and the entire Church. Mary is the example *par excellence* of this, and through her maternal care can we offer ourselves more perfectly to her Son.

- How can I offer my sufferings to Christ through the Immaculata today?
- Are there any particular obstacles to my docility to the Holy Spirit that I can take active steps to remove?

After the Reflection, pray the Marian Prayers the *Sub Tuum Præsidium*, the *Hail Mary*, and the *Hail Holy Queen.*

Day 21

Mary, Our Advocate

"It is as if a peasant, wishing to gain the friendship and benevolence of the king, went to the queen, and presented her with a fruit, which was his whole revenue, in order that she might present it to the king. The queen, having accepted the poor little offering from the peasant, would place the fruit on a large and beautiful dish of gold, and so, on the peasant's behalf, would present it to the king. Then the fruit, however unworthy in itself to be a king's present, would become worthy of his majesty, because of the dish of gold on which it rested and the person who presented it."[8]

–St. Louis de Montfort, True Devotion to Mary

Above St. Louis de Montfort describes by analogy what it is like when we give the offerings we desire to give to God to Mary. She is not the end recipient of our gifts, because they are

---

[8] Louis de Montfort, *True Devotion to the Blessed Virgin*, para. 147, trans. Frederick William
Faber, https://www.ecatholic2000.com/montfort/true/devotion.shtml

meant for God. But we give them to her so that she might present them to her Son on our behalf. By making them her own offerings, de Montfort says, "She embellishes our works, adorning them with her own merits and virtues."

You might be asking yourself why your offerings need to be purified if Jesus died on the Cross to elevate us and invite us into a participation in the inner life of the Trinity, and to that I would like to present two points:

1. Although through Baptism we are made a new creation as children of God, we still suffer some of the effects of Original Sin. We have concupiscence (that is, the attachment to sin), we struggle with at least venial sins daily—and oftentimes these venial sins are done deliberately, and finally because even with our good intentions our actions are laced with self-love.

By self-love, we refer to the secret pride we have within ourselves. We might not know that we are acting out of pride, but it is very difficult to get to a place where we are entirely resigned to God's will rather than ours, and that we do our actions without any speck of wanting a reward. Also, by self-love, we are referring to a disordered love of self, not the love that is a fitting response to God's gift of life and His creating us in His image and likeness. Overcoming this type of pride is an ongoing journey, which takes time and acts of discipline and self-denial. We continuously try to become more conformed to God's will, and in this we need grace and the help of the Immaculata.

2. Our Lady is perfectly united to God and His will, she is perfected by grace from her Immaculate Conception, and she is the one who sits at the right hand of her Son in the Heavenly Kingdom as the *Gebirah*—the one whose job it is to hear the petitions of those in the Kingdom and present them to her Son.

When Mary offers our gifts to her Son and her own gifts, how would He deny them? He accepts them as loving gifts from His Mother, and this loving acceptance is thus given to us. (Yes, Christ accepts us as children of God, but that doesn't mean every one of our prayers is acceptable to Him—remember we are fallen and often want things that are not good for us.)

As a note, when we make petitions to Mary that are not in line with God's will, her purification of our offerings still obtains for us those things which we truly need. Not only does she obtain for us those things which we need for our salvation, but as we see in the example of the Wedding at Cana, she intercedes even for our temporal needs—she is our Mother who desires to bless her children.

Mary's Intercession Omnipotent by Grace

It bears repeating that it is God's will to use creatures to accomplish His will. He wants us to be involved in our salvation, and as such has established a Church with a hierarchy. Rather than leaving us a Bible with instructions on how to simply have a personal relationship with Him, He established an entire family, where members have their roles and help each other into the Kingdom. Priests hear our Confessions and bring us the Eucharist, bishops do the same and shepherd their respective dioceses, and the Communion of Saints prays for one another, especially in the powerful intercession of the saints in heaven. We clearly see this in Revelation when, "the four living creatures and the twenty-four elders fell down before the Lamb, each holding a harp, and with golden bowls full of incense, which are the prayers of the saints" (Revelation 5:8).

The Immaculata is the one who is perfectly united to the Spirit, whose will has been so formed into His that it is as if they have one will (really this is a perfect union of two, but it is so close we could never perceive any division). Every single thing she prays for, she receives a "yes" in response. As our spiritual Mother, Mary never despises any prayer from her children. She always hears us and brings our needs to her Son.

Reflection

The Power of Marian Consecration is that by the act of self-giving to Mary, we ask her to aid us in our needs for our entire lives. Even when we do not perceive that we need something, by our total consecration we have an open line of request to her to fly to our assistance in times of need. As the Mother of the Church, she does this anyways, praying always for our needs, but in Marian consecration we give her permission to exercise that role more fully in our lives.

- Do I have any reservations to giving Mary all of my offerings to give to her Son?
- How can I relinquish control to the Immaculata today, and as such experience a deeper peace in my spiritual life?

After the Reflection, pray the Marian Prayers the *Sub Tuum Præsidium,* the *Hail Mary,* and the *Hail Holy Queen.*

Day 22

The Wedding at Cana

"His mother said to the servants, 'Do whatever he tells you.'"

–John 2:5

The Wedding at Cana is a familiar story: a couple is getting married and Mary, Jesus, and his disciples are invited. Wedding feasts of that time lasted for days rather than hours, and it was the duty of the hosts of the wedding to provide enough food and drink for their guests. At this particular wedding, the unthinkable happened: they ran out of wine. This would have been a huge embarrassment for the couple, but instead it becomes the beginning of Christ's public ministry.

Mary's Role at the Wedding at Cana

When this story is retold, people often say how when the couple ran out of wine, someone ran up to Mary to ask her assistance in the matter. But if we read closely, we do not ever see this occur. It may have happened, but it is also possible—and honestly very likely—that Mary saw for herself that the couple had run out of wine and took it upon herself to come to their assistance. We know the rest of the story—she goes to Jesus and tells Him of the dilemma, Jesus responds in perhaps peculiar language (that we will discuss in just a moment), and then Mary proceeds to tell the servants to do whatever her Son tells them to do, knowing that He will take care of their needs.

Christ then has the servants fill large basins with water—those typically used for washing so as to follow the Jewish purification laws. Scholars estimate that Jesus provided around 180 gallons of choice vintage wine. This was so noticeable that the chief steward of the feast questioned why the good wine was saved until now.

Mary knew this would happen. She exemplifies her role as Advocate and intercessor here, and in such a way that is loaded with symbolism. Firstly, this takes place at a wedding. Mary brings a need to her Son on behalf of a couple at their wedding, initiating Christ's public ministry. This is important because the climax of salvation history is the Wedding Feast of the Lamb in the book of Revelation. We participate as members of the Church, which is the Bride of Christ. All of Christ's ministry is to bring the God's wandering people to Him as His Bride.

Secondly, Christ responds initially to Mary in these words, "O woman, what have you to do with me? My hour has not yet come" (John 2:4). You might think that Jesus is rebuffing her, but, in actuality, he is highlighting something important. In the Gospel of John, the "hour" speaks of Christ's Passion and Death on the Cross. Here Mary is setting in motion the path that leads to Calvary—it starts at one wedding and leads to the moment where Christ's eternal covenant is consummated on the Cross ("It is consummated" is a translation of John 19:30).

Jesus, in calling His Mother "woman" is identifying her with the woman of Genesis 3:15, knowing that she is the one who participates with Him in ushering in the redemption. Just as Eve offered the fruit to Adam which led to the Fall, Mary intercedes for Jesus to provide the fruit of the vine for the wedding feast, beginning His ministry of our salvation. Then at the Cross, Jesus looks down at Our Lady standing with St. John and calls her again, "woman."

Mary and Our Needs

Just as Mary saw the need of the wedding couple before being asked, Mary sees our needs, too. She runs to her Son with those things we require for our salvation and even with things meant simply to bless us. The couple at the wedding feast needed the temporal good of wine for their wedding—Mary cared enough to simply save a couple from embarrassment, she does the same for us. Our Lady has a tender Mother's heart that aches when we ache. She wants her children to be blessed and cared for. The ultimate care is our salvation, but know that you have a Mother who cares for all your needs.

Reflection

When Mary hears of our needs, there are a couple of things that result: first she brings our petitions to her Son with the same expectancy for an answer she had at Cana (but now with knowledge instead of faith because she has the Beatific Vision), knowing she will get an answer, and second, that she looks to us with our instructions for receiving the answer to our prayers: "Do whatever he tells you."

- Do I go to Mary with even the smallest needs I have? The ones that may seem trivial?
- Do I trust that Mary cares about every one of my needs? From the most mundane, to the most severe?

After the Reflection, pray the Marian Prayers the *Sub Tuum Præsidium,* the *Hail Mary,* and the *Hail Holy Queen.*

Day 23

The Militia Immaculatae

"The essential condition for membership in the Militia of the Immaculata is consecration to the Blessed Immaculate Virgin Mary, in order to become, in her immaculate hands, instruments for the conversion and sanctification of the greatest possible number of souls.
Your activities must be not only 'defensive' but also above all 'offensive.'"[9]

–St. Maximilian Kolbe

One of the greatest modern Marian saints is without a doubt St. Maximilian Kolbe. Many know of his heroic sacrifice in offering his life for another in Auschwitz, but far too few know of his tireless work in spreading devotion to the Immaculata.

As a precocious young child, St. Maximilian (born Rajmund Kolbe), was rambunctious and very bright. As many

---

[9] Maximilian Kolbe, "1031 A Reply," in *The Writings of St. Maximilian Maria Kolbe*, vol. 2, *Various Writings* (Lugano, Italy: Nerbini International, 2016), 1838.

of you parents out there know, this combination can be a recipe for trouble! One day when young Kolbe was acting rather unrestrained, his mother yelled at him, "What is to become of you, Rajmund?!" Stricken by this question, he went to his local parish, St. Matthew's, and prayed, asking Our Lady that very question. It was there that the Blessed Virgin Mary appeared to him offering him two crowns: a red crown for martyrdom and a white crown for purity. The bold Kolbe accepted without hesitation.

This pivotal moment set the course for Kolbe's life, taking the name Maximilian as a Franciscan Friar because he funneled his energy towards the greatest things, wanting to run at full speed, giving the maximum in serving the Immaculata and thus Jesus Christ. This is clearly seen in the event of the 200th anniversary of Freemasonry in 1917. Kolbe was studying in Rome and witnessed a shocking display of hostility toward the Church. Freemasons marched through the streets waving their banners which Kolbe called "rags" containing images of Lucifer trampling over St. Michael the Archangel while they were shouting blasphemies against the Holy Father. Kolbe even recounts reading the phrase, "The devil will rule in the Vatican and the Pope will be his Swiss Guard."

For Maximilian, this was no ordinary provocation—it was a call to arms. Despite wanting to be a soldier in his youth, he did not take up a sword or raise a political movement. Instead, he formed a spiritual army under the Queen of Heaven: the *Militia Immaculatae*—the Militia of the Immaculata.

Under the Banner of the Immaculata

In 1917, Kolbe united his brother friars to enlist in his militia. If the enemies of the Church could rally under the banner of the serpent, then the children of Mary must unite beneath the banner of the Immaculata. The battle was not against flesh and blood but against the powers and principalities opposed to God (cf. Eph 6:12). His aim was not destruction but conversion—to win the whole world for Christ through the Immaculata—seeking the consecration of every soul who lives in the present and who will live in the future. He understood that the surest and most powerful way to bring souls to God was through consecration to Mary, for through her came the Savior Himself. The more people he could enlist into her service, the greater her army would become, and through her, the head of the serpent would be crushed (cf. Gn 3:15).

The program of the MI was simple: to extend the Blessed Kingdom of the Most Sacred Heart of Jesus as far as possible as soon as possible through total consecration to the Immaculata focusing on two primary points:

> The two sentences at the beginning of the program, "She will strike at your head" (cf. Gn 3:15) and "You alone have destroyed all heresies in the whole world" (Office of the B.V.M.), also indicate the purpose of the Militia. Therefore the members of the MI consecrate themselves to the Immaculata without limits as instruments in her hand, that through them she may deign to achieve what is expressed in those two sentences.[10]

We win this battle not by destroying our enemies, but by winning them over to our side. As Kolbe continued:

---

[10] Maximilian Kolbe, "1046 About the Militia of the Immaculata," in *The Writings of St. Maximilian Maria Kolbe*, vol. 2, *Various Writings* (Lugano, Italy: Nerbini International, 2016), 1854–1855.

> Moreover, says that she has destroyed 'heresies' not 'heretics,' because she loves them and loves them very much. For she is the best mother: because of that she rescues them from the darkness of falsehood and from the snares of evil, destroying the powers of hell. Our goal, therefore, is 'to engage in the work of converting sinners, heretics, schismatics, etc.; but above all the Freemasons, and to strive toward the sanctification of everyone, under the protection and through the mediation of the Immaculata.'[11]

Kolbe knew that it was only by surrendering ourselves over to the Immaculata, by giving ourselves to her as her property and possession, that we can quickly and easily be made saints and instruments in the immaculate hands of the Virgin. This is how we allow her to crush the head of the infernal serpent in our lives and in the world around us.

We can all fight in this battle, of which each of us is a part today. It starts in our homes, in the quiet of our hearts, in the busyness of our schedules. When we make the act of consecration to Mary, we become soldiers protected under her mantle. We seek to accomplish the two goals of the Militia Immaculata—the crush the head of the serpent and destroy all heresies. Effectively this means to extend the Kingdom of God by winning souls into the Church.

Reflection

This sounds like a tall order, but our participation is simple (not easy): to give oneself to Mary and live that consecration through prayer and fidelity. The requirements

---

[11] Ibid., 1855.

Kolbe set forth for the militia are simply to consecrate to Mary, to wear the Miraculous Medal (which we will discuss in a later reflection) and to say the Miraculous Medal prayer each day. He further compared the Miraculous Medal to a bullet, and the Rosary to a sword in the hand of the Knights of the Immaculata. To be consecrated to Mary is to allow her to act through us, to make us docile instruments in the ongoing battle for souls.

- Pray the Miraculous Medal Prayer: "O Mary, conceived without sin, pray for us who have recourse to thee."
- Am I discouraged or anxious at the thought of participating in the Immaculata's spiritual battle for the salvation of souls? How can I give Mary my concerns today to allow her to crush the head of the serpent in my life?

After the Reflection, pray the Marian Prayers the *Sub Tuum Præsidium*, the *Hail Mary*, and the *Hail Holy Queen.*

Day 24

The Joint Mission of Mary and the Holy Spirit

> *"The Third Person of the Most Holy Trinity also participates in this work [of redemption], since by virtue of the redemption accomplished by Christ, He transforms the souls of men into temples of God: He makes us adoptive children of God and heirs of the kingdom of heaven. St. Paul, in fact, states: "You have been washed, [...] justified in the name of our Lord Jesus Christ and in the Spirit of our God" [1 Cor 6:11]."*[12]
>
> *–St. Maximilian Kolbe*

We have spoken thus far about the Immaculata's relationship with the Holy Spirit as her indissoluble Spouse—that she takes for herself the name "Immaculate Conception"

---

[12] Maximilian Kolbe, "1229 The Immaculate Conception of the Blessed Virgin Mary in Relation to the Mediation of All Graces," in *The Writings of St. Maximilian Maria Kolbe*, vol. 2, *Various Writings* (Lugano, Italy: Nerbini International, 2016), 2133.

after the Holy Spirit who is, as St. Maximilian Kolbe describes, the "Uncreated Immaculate Conception." This relationship reveals Mary's potency in her participation in the redemption with her Son and thus leads to her ongoing mediation. This can all seem a bit complicated, or perhaps out of reach, so it is important for us to take a closer look at who the Holy Spirit is, and at the joint mission which He shares with His Beloved Spouse, the Immaculate Virgin Mary.

Who is the Holy Spirit?

The Holy Spirit is the Counselor, the Advocate sent to us after Pentecost. He is the one who empowered the Apostles to change from timid, uneducated men to bold, confident proclaimers of the Gospel. We likewise receive this transformation in our Baptism and Confirmation, where the Holy Spirit changes us into children of God and fills us with the sanctifying grace necessary to go forth as disciples of Christ.

F.X. Durrwell, in his book, "The Holy Spirit of God" describes the Holy Spirit as the "action of God." This is a difficult thought to grasp—He is a Person who is Himself divine action. We clearly see in Scripture that Christ performed miracles by the "finger of God" or the "hand of God"—both of which are biblical titles which refer to the Holy Spirit. The Spirit is the power by which Christ performed every miracle and healing. It is the Spirit that hovered over the waters of creation when God brought something out of nothing.

Durrwell described the Spirit as this action which ebbs and flows, like the waves that crash against the shore and rebound back to the sea. The wave has a certain power and an impact but itself cannot be grasped or contained, for it flows back out and disperses. The Spirit has this type of action with us—flowing towards us with God's grace and pulling us back into His transforming love. Each time the Spirit moves, He brings us more inward, into our inner lives of prayer, into the life of the Blessed Trinity. We see this mirrored in Our Lady, who pondered the mysteries of God in her heart. She remained quiet in prayer, filled with the Spirit.

The Fathers of the Church called the Holy Spirit the *font of all holiness*. Holy, or Immaculate, if His very name. He is the sanctifier. As we see in Scripture, when God gave new names to people when He gave them particular tasks, the Holy Spirit's name indicates to us what He does and who He is. He is the one who sanctifies us so that we can grow in the love of God. He is Love itself—the fruitful Love between the Father and the Son.

Love Gone Forth

St. Kolbe puts it beautifully in describing the Spirit's cooperation with Mary in bringing this love into human history:

> The Holy Spirit, who is infertile within the Trinity, because no Divine Person proceeds from Him, became fruitful through Mary, whom He chose as His bride. With her, in her, and through her He realizes His masterpiece, that is to say, the Word incarnate. 'The Holy Spirit shall come upon thee, and the power of the Most High shall overshadow thee' [Lk 1:35]. That, however, should not be understood to mean that the Blessed Virgin gave the Holy Spirit the fruitfulness that He, as God, would have to have, like the Father and the Son, even though in fact He did not put it to fruition, for the simple reason that no divine Person proceeds from Him. Rather, we should understand it in the

> sense that the Holy Spirit resolved to use the mediation of Mary, while having absolutely no need of it in order to manifest His own fertility, forming through her and with her the human nature of Christ.
>
> Even after Christ's death the Holy Spirit works all things in us through Mary. In fact, what the Creator said to the serpent in reference to the Immaculata, "She will crush your head" [cf. Gn 3:15], is, according to the teaching of theologians, to be understood to have no limitations of time.
>
> It is the task of the Holy Spirit to form the new members of those predestined to the Mystical Body of Christ until the end of the world. But, as Blessed Louis Grignion demonstrates, this work is brought to fruition with Mary, in Mary, and through Mary.[13]

In short, the Holy Spirit's mission is to make us holy. He is the one sent to form God's love deeply within us. Mary partakes intimately in this mission; the two inseparable spouses carry out their namesake—the created and uncreated Immaculate Conception—drawing us closer to becoming immaculate through growth in holiness.

Reflection

The Holy Spirit was sent to us at Pentecost, enlivening the Church and filling her with power. It is peculiar that through the history of the Church there are more recorded

---

[13] Ibid., 2134.

Marian apparitions than apparitions of Jesus. Could this be because the Holy Spirit is working through Mary to bring us to her Son, and this is God's will to use the Immaculata to bring us to Him? As such, Marian apparitions are just as much a work of the Holy Spirit as they are of Our Lady.

- What consistent themes do I see across Marian apparitions?
- Given the consistency of messages from Marian apparitions and that Mary's entire mission is to make each of us holy, what common practices can I adopt to grow in holiness?

After the Reflection, pray the Marian Prayers the *Sub Tuum Præsidium,* the *Hail Mary,* and the *Hail Holy Queen.*

Day 25

Our Lady of the Rosary

"You see the wonderful results I have had in preaching the Holy Rosary. You and those who love Our Lady must do the same; through the holy devotion of the Rosary, you will attract all to the true science of the virtues."

—*St. Dominic*

The Rosary is one of the greatest treasures of the Catholic spiritual life—simple, profound, and powerful beyond measure. Throughout history, it has been called a "spiritual weapon" against evil, a chain binding the devil, and a "compendium of the Gospel." Its aim is simple—to help us penetrate the divine mysteries by meditating upon the life of Christ while asking the intercession of the Blessed Virgin for assistance. As we clutch the beads, we take the hand of our Blessed Mother, and she walks with us, leading us directly to her Son. We take after her example, she who pondered all these things in her heart, while her powerful intercession opens us to receive the many graces and blessings that the Holy Spirit has to bestow upon us.

St. Maximilian Kolbe called the Rosary a "sword in the hand of the Knight of the Immaculata," and St. Padre Pio called it a "weapon for our times." Following the thought of Kolbe, that the way to win the spiritual battle was through union with Christ through the Immaculata, the Rosary becomes a powerful tool by which the Immaculata crushes the head of the serpent and helps us to truly encounter Christ in the depths of prayer.

The History of the Rosary

Tradition tells us that the Rosary was given by the Blessed Virgin to St. Dominic in the thirteenth century. At the time, the Church was being afflicted by the Albigensian heresy—a revival of ancient Manichaeism that rejected the material world as evil and denied the Incarnation. Dominic, called to preach against these errors, struggled to convert hearts hardened by falsehood. In his distress, he turned to the Mother of God, who appeared to him and entrusted him with a new method of preaching: to proclaim the mysteries of salvation while leading the faithful to meditate on them through the recitation of the "Angelic Salutation"—the Hail Mary. The Rosary, then, was not merely a prayer but a catechesis—a way of preaching the Gospel through contemplation.

And it bore fruit. The Rosary rekindled faith, renewed hope, and drew countless souls back to the truth—even miraculously. Since that time, the Church has seen again and again the miraculous power of the Rosary against evil. It was clearly seen that the Rosary was a means by which the head of the serpent was crushed, and Mary destroyed the heresies of the world—for she always brings clarification of our understanding of her Son and leads us to more perfect faith in Him.

The most famous example of the power of the Rosary is perhaps the Battle of Lepanto in 1571, when Christian forces were vastly outnumbered by the Ottoman fleet. Pope St. Pius V called all of Europe to pray the Rosary for victory. When the Christian fleet triumphed against impossible odds, the Pope attributed the victory to Our Lady's intercession and established the feast of Our Lady of the Rosary (at the time called Our Lady of Victory) on October 7th in gratitude.

Then at Fatima in 1917, Our Lady identified herself as the "Lady of the Rosary." She called the world to conversion and prayer—specifically through the daily recitation of the Rosary—promising that this would bring about a great peace. The children she appeared to were simple shepherds, but through them she gave a message to the modern world: that the Rosary is the remedy for sin, war, and unbelief. "Pray the Rosary every day," she said, "to obtain peace for the world and the end of the war." The weapon St. Dominic wielded against heresy became the same weapon to confront the godlessness of the twentieth century—and remains the same weapon today.

Pope St. Pius X, often called the Pope of the Eucharist, also recognized the Rosary's power. He granted countless indulgences to those who prayed it devoutly, insisting that true recitation of the Rosary must involve both vocal prayer and meditation. It is not a mechanical repetition but a contemplative exercise that unites word and meditation. This is especially important: we should not race through the Rosary, we should focus on the mysteries. The end goal of any kind of meditation is to become more united to Christ, and to allow Him to transform our hearts. This is especially true of Marian devotion, including the Rosary: Mary always points us to Christ.

Reflection

I would argue that the prayers of the Church ladies who devoutly show up each day to pray the Rosary before Mass strengthen the Church in such a way that may come close to those cloistered religious priests and nuns. But it must be said that the Rosary is not meant only for them! You are called to pray the Rosary! Pick up your spiritual sword and pray it. It is a wonderful way to stay rooted in Scripture so as to not fall into the warning of St. Jerome, "He who is ignorant of Scripture is ignorant of Christ."

The Rosary is a treasure waiting for you, through which Our Lady will crush the head of the serpent in your life and lead you to the Truth, who is her Son, Jesus Christ.

In the next reflection, we will discuss how to pray the Rosary and explore its mysteries in greater detail.

- Have I ever prayed the Rosary? Try to pray at least one decade (one mystery composed of one *Our Father*, ten *Hail Marys*, and one *Glory Be*) today.
- What is keeping me from praying the Rosary each day? Can I rearrange my schedule to prioritize it?

After the Reflection, pray the Marian Prayers the *Sub Tuum Præsidium*, the *Hail Mary*, and the *Hail Holy Queen*

Day 26

How to Pray the Rosary

"THE ROSARY is made up of two things: mental prayer and vocal prayer. In the Holy Rosary mental prayer is none other than meditation of the chief mysteries of the life, death and glory of Jesus Christ and if His Blessed Mother. Vocal prayer consists in saying fifteen decades of the Hail Mary, each decade headed by an Our Father."[14]

—St. Louis de Montfort

The Rosary is not merely a series of repetitive prayers; it is a school of contemplation, a way of entering into the life of Christ through the eyes and heart of His Mother. To pray the Rosary well is to walk with Mary through the Gospel, meditating upon the mysteries of our salvation.

---

[14] de Montfort, St. Louis. *The Secret of the Rosary.* Translated by Mary Barbour. New York: Montfort Publications, 1954. https://www.ecatholic2000.com/montfort/rosary/rosary.shtml

The Two Parts

Our introductory quote for this reflection tells us that the Rosary is a combination of vocal prayer and meditation. The physical rosary beads are at the service of the vocal prayers, and our vocal prayer serves the meditation component during which we meditate upon the lives of Christ and the Virgin Mary. The prayers of each decade both request the intercession of the Immaculata and act as spiritual rhythm, ensuring we spend at least a certain amount of time in meditation of each mystery.

As St. Louis de Montfort explains, the Rosary "is a priceless treasure inspired by God." Through repetition, our lips speak the Angelic salutation—the words of the Archangel Gabriel, "Hail, full of grace! The Lord is with thee!" and the words of St. Elizabeth, "Blessed is the fruit of thy womb!" while Mary mediates Christ's presence to us just as she did in the Visitation to Elizabeth and John the Baptist in her womb.

The meditation upon the mysteries is not a mere thought of what happened—although that is an important component. To truly meditate is to see with the heart, to enter the mystery and place yourself within it alongside Jesus and Mary. It is not so important to think much as to love much.

How to Pray the Rosary

The Rosary begins with the recitation of the Apostles' Creed and is followed by an Our Father for the intentions of the Pope, three Hail Marys said for an increase in the virtues of faith, hope and love, then a Glory Be. After these introductory prayers, the first mystery is announced, followed by one Our Father, ten Hail Marys, one Glory Be, and the optional Fatima Prayer. This process is repeated five times to cover a set of five mysteries of the Rosary. The Rosary concludes then with the Hail Holy Queen and some optional closing prayers.

Traditionally, there are fifteen mysteries, grouped in three sets: the Joyful, the Sorrowful, and the Glorious. In 2002, Pope St. John Paul II added a fourth set—the Luminous Mysteries—to contemplate the public ministry of Christ. Each set invites us to meditate on a different aspect of the Gospel, revealing the full pattern of redemption. Below is the list of the different mysteries of the Rosary accompanied by the traditional days in which they are prayed and relevant Scripture verses for each.

The Joyful Mysteries (Prayed on Mondays and Saturdays)

1. The Annunciation (Luke 1:26–38)
2. The Visitation (Luke 1:39–56)
3. The Nativity (Luke 2:1–20)
4. The Presentation of Christ in the Temple (Luke 2:22–38)
5. The Finding of the Child Jesus in the Temple (Luke 2:41–52)

The Luminous Mysteries (Prayed on Thursdays)

1. The Baptism of the Lord (Matthew 3:13–17)
2. The Wedding at Cana (John 2:1–12)
3. The Proclamation of the Kingdom (Mark 1:14–15)
4. The Transfiguration (Matthew 17:1–8)
5. The Institution of the Eucharist (Luke 22:19–20)

The Sorrowful Mysteries (Prayed on Tuesdays and Fridays)

1. The Agony in the Garden (Luke 22:39–46)
2. The Scourging at the Pillar (John 19:1)

3. The Crowning with Thorns (Mark 15:16–20)
4. The Carrying of the Cross (John 19:17)
5. The Crucifixion and Death of Christ (Luke 23:44–46)

The Glorious Mysteries (Prayed on Wednesdays and Sundays)

1. The Resurrection (Matthew 28:1–10)
2. The Ascension of Christ into Heaven (Acts 1:6–11)
3. The Descent of the Holy Spirit (Acts 2:1–4)
4. The Assumption of Mary (Psalm 132:8)
5. The Coronation of Mary (Revelation 12:1)

Reflection

When you pray the Rosary, begin by placing yourself in the presence of God. Offer your Rosary for a particular intention or person. As you take the beads in hand, remember that Mary is with you—your Mother, guide, and intercessor.

Take note that eighteen of the twenty mysteries are directly about the life of Christ, and the remaining two show of Mary's perfect discipleship to Him. In this way, the Rosary becomes what St. John Paul II called "a compendium of the Gospel." Every mystery is a window into the redemptive love of Christ. Through it, Mary leads us to her Son and intercedes for us, helping to prepare our hearts to receive the gifts merited by Christ, of which St. Bernardine says: "All the gifts, graces, virtues of the Holy Spirit are distributed by the hands of Mary, to whom she wills, when she wills, as she wills, and in the measure she wills." The Rosary is the powerful means of grace, opening our hearts to these divine gifts.

- Do I own a Rosary? Where is it? (Go grab it now and keep it on your person.)
- What is something I desperately need an answer to in prayer to right now? Pray the Rosary for that intention.

After the Reflection, pray the Marian Prayers the *Sub Tuum Præsidium,* the *Hail Mary,* and the *Hail Holy Queen.*

Day 27

Mary: First and Most Perfect Disciple

> *"In fact, each and every one of us has to be concerned only with this: to harmonize, conform, merge our will completely with the will of the Immaculata, as much as her will is completely united with God's, and her heart with the Heart of her Son Jesus."*[15]
>
> *–St. Maximilian Kolbe*

When we speak of discipleship, we often think of those who uprooted their lives at the call of Jesus to follow Him—St. Peter and Andrew leaving their nets, Matthew leaving his booth as a tax collector, and John resting his head upon the breast of Jesus. Yet before all of them, Mary had already given herself completely to God's will, long before she beheld the physical face of her Son. Father Reginald Garrigou-Lagrange wrote that the two most essential things for the spiritual life are to hear the

---

[15] Maximilian Kolbe, "1160 Our War," in *The Writings of St. Maximilian Maria Kolbe*, vol. 2, *Various Writings* (Lugano, Italy: Nerbini International, 2016), 2011.

Word of God and live by it. Mary is the first and most perfect disciple because not only did she hear, but she received the Word of God in the flesh into her womb, and not only did she live by the Word, but she lived in perfect conformity with Him and with His will.

The Fiat of Discipleship

At the Annunciation, when the angel Gabriel greeted her with words that kickstarted the events of our salvation—"Hail, full of grace, the Lord is with you"—Mary did not hesitate. Her response was not one of doubt, but of wonder: "How can this be, since I know not man?" When she received the answer that the Holy Spirit would overshadow her, she gave her total assent: "Behold, I am the handmaid of the Lord; let it be done to me according to your word."

In that moment, Mary became the model of every disciple. Discipleship begins with hearing, accepting, and responding. Her "yes" was not a one-time act but an exclamation of the orientation of her entire life. Her will was conformed to God's, allowing the Word to become flesh within her for the sake of our salvation.

Evangelization and the Magnificat

Immediately we see that Mary begins to embody the call that Christ would later give His disciples to preach the Gospel to all nations. In the actions of Mary who "arose and went with haste" (Luke 1:39) to her kinswoman Elizabeth, she was already bringing the very Word of God out into the world, mediating His presence to Elizabeth and John the Baptist in the womb.

Mary's words in the Magnificat reveal the heart of a true disciple, exemplified by humility, gratitude, and faith: "My soul magnifies the Lord, and my spirit rejoices in God my Savior, for he has regarded the low estate of his handmaiden. For behold, henceforth all generations will call me blessed" (Luke 1:46–48).

Mary does not glorify herself, even though she has been exalted above every other creature. Her joy is not in what she has done, but in what God has done through her. This is the essence of discipleship: to magnify the Lord, not ourselves. Her humility is not self-deprecation but the truth—the truth that all we are and all we have comes from Him.

Inward Meditation, Outward Action

We know that prayer is meant to change us. Through prayer, we are transformed and conformed to God. The fire of God's love purges us of all our imperfections and unites us more deeply to Himself. This transformation ultimately leads to external actions—we receive God's love and grace, and it flows through us, leading us to spread it throughout the world.

Our Lady is the most perfect example of this. Although she did not need any purification due to sin, the fire of God's love filled her and continuously deepened her union with her divine Son. This is evidenced in her continual meditation on the mysteries of God, as St. Luke said of Mary following the Birth of Jesus (cf. Luke 2:19) and after finding the Child Jesus, after losing Him in the Temple for three days, Mary "kept all these things in her heart" (Luke 2:51).

Mary's faith then led to actions that furthered the Kingdom of God. She interceded for the first public miracle of her Son at the wedding at Cana, telling those there and all of us, "Do whatever he tells you" (John 2:5); she stood by her Son at the foot of the Cross, sharing in His sufferings (cf. John 19); and she prayed with the disciples awaiting the coming of the Holy Spirit at Pentecost.

Discipleship Even to the Cross

Mary's discipleship reached its perfection at the foot of the Cross. There, where others fled, she remained. She shared not only in His suffering, but in His offering, fulfilling what was foreshadowed by Abraham and Isaac—Mary, as Lumen Gentium states, stood at the Cross "uniting herself with a maternal heart with His sacrifice, and lovingly consenting to the immolation of this Victim which she herself had brought forth." She stood as the New Eve beside the New Adam, uniting her heart to His perfect obedience unto death. In that moment, her discipleship led to her becoming the spiritual Mother of the Church: "Woman, behold your son."

To be a disciple of Christ means to stand with Mary at the Cross. It means to unite our sufferings to His, to persevere when others turn away, and to receive from Christ the same gift John received—to take Mary into our own homes and our own lives.

Reflection

Mary's entire life is the pattern of what it means to follow Jesus. Her obedience at the Annunciation, her humility in the Magnificat, her silence in suffering, her perseverance at the Cross—each reveals a soul completely given over to God.

In order to become true disciples like Mary, we need her help. Grace is absolutely necessary for this transformation to take place within us. When we entrust ourselves to her—through daily prayer, consecration, and imitation—she forms us into the likeness of her Son.

- In what practical ways can I imitate Mary's discipleship according to my state in life?

- What particular sufferings do I encounter that I can, in union with Mary, unite to the sufferings of Christ?

After the Reflection, pray the Marian Prayers the *Sub Tuum Præsidium*, the *Hail Mary*, and the *Hail Holy Queen.*

Day 28

The Ten Virtues of Mary

"True devotion to our Lady is holy, that is, it leads us to avoid sin and to imitate the virtues of Mary. Her ten principal virtues are: deep humility, lively faith, blind obedience, unceasing prayer, constant self-denial, surpassing purity, ardent love, heroic patience, angelic kindness, and heavenly wisdom."[16]

–St. Louis de Montfort

St. Louis de Montfort, in *True Devotion to Mary,* tells us that true devotion to Our Lady is not merely external or sentimental—it is transformative. He writes that genuine devotion to the Blessed Virgin "is holy, that is, it leads us to avoid sin and to imitate the virtues of Mary." He then lists ten principal virtues of the Immaculata: deep humility, lively faith, blind obedience, unceasing prayer, constant self-denial, surpassing purity, ardent love, heroic patience, angelic kindness, and heavenly wisdom.

---

[16] St. Louis de Montfort, *The Secret of Mary* (New York: Montfort Publications, 1954), https://www.ecatholic2000.com/montfort/secret/secret.shtml

If we truly love Mary, we will not only honor her but strive to imitate her. These virtues describe the interior life of the Blessed Virgin—her heart, perfectly conformed to God's will. To draw close to her Son, we must learn to live as she lived, allowing her virtues to take root in our souls and allowing her to guide our actions in imitating them.

1. **Deep Humility**
   Chosen to be the Mother of God, Mary called herself the "handmaid of the Lord." Her greatness lay in her littleness, which magnified God's greatness. We imitate her humility when we acknowledge that all good in us comes from God alone. True humility leads us to see ourselves as utterly dependent on grace.

2. **Lively Faith**
   Mary's faith was alive and steadfast. She believed the angel's word even when reason could not explain it. Her faith endured through silence and suffering, especially at the Cross. We imitate her faith when we trust God's promises in the dark, knowing that He is faithful.

3. **Blind Obedience**
   Mary's *fiat*—"let it be done to me according to your word"—was total surrender. Her obedience was not foolish, but born of trust. We imitate her when we obey God promptly, even when we do not understand His plan. True obedience unites our will to His.

4. **Unceasing Prayer**
   Mary's heart was always turned toward and united to God. Whether at Nazareth or Calvary, her life was a living prayer, pondering the mysteries of God in her

heart. We imitate this by seeking God's presence throughout the day, turning every joy and sorrow into prayer. The Rosary teaches us this rhythm of communion with Jesus through Mary.

5. **Constant Self-Denial**
   Mary lived entirely for God, offering herself in silence and love. We imitate her by denying ourselves—not in bitterness, but in love. Each act of self-denial prepares room for grace, making our souls empty of self and filled with God.

6. **Surpassing Purity**
   Mary's purity was total integrity of heart—every thought and desire ordered to God. Purity means loving God with an undivided heart, not allowing anything else to occupy space in that heart, and only loving created things as gifts from God that point us back to Him (love of neighbor is also an extension of love of God, not a love given apart from Him). We imitate her by guarding our senses and striving for interior chastity. Purity brings clarity; when our hearts are clean, we see God more clearly.

7. **Ardent Love**
   Mary's heart burned with divine charity. Everything she did—from daily chores (especially in raising the Christ Child) to standing beneath the Cross—was an act of love. We imitate her when our love for God overflows into service and sacrifice. To love as Mary loved is to give our hearts without reserve.

8. **Heroic Patience**

Mary endured misunderstanding, poverty, and the agony of Calvary without complaint. We imitate her patience when we bear our trials with peace, trusting that God's providence is at work. Heroic patience is active trust in the midst of suffering, relying completely on God to bring about the best outcome—
His will.

9. **Angelic Kindness**
   Every encounter with Mary reveals her gentleness. She brought peace wherever she went (and continues to mediate Christ's presence, which is true peace—think back to Mary mediating Christ to Elizabeth and John the Baptist). We imitate her by speaking kindly, acting gently, and treating every soul with dignity. Kindness evangelizes—it is the fragrance of sanctity that endures even the harshest treatment with grace. (Imitating this virtue does not mean being a pacifist, but means maintaining peace and Christian charity even when doing the right thing in difficult situations.)

10. **Heavenly Wisdom**
    Mary pondered all things in her heart, seeing them through God's light. Her wisdom was not intellectual pride, but the fruit of contemplation. We imitate her by seeking God's wisdom through prayer and Scripture, learning to see as God sees.

Reflection

Mary embodies these virtues perfectly because she is perfectly united to the Holy Spirit, the font of all holiness. When we consecrate ourselves to her, we invite her to form these same virtues in us—to teach us to live as she lived and to love as she loved. If we let her guide us, she will draw us ever closer to the heart of God.

- Which virtue do I have the easiest time imitating?
- Which virtue is hardest for me to exercise? How can I actively work on growing in that virtue?

After the Reflection, pray the Marian Prayers the *Sub Tuum Præsidium,* the *Hail Mary,* and the *Hail Holy Queen.*

Day 29

The Seven Sorrows and Seven Joys of Mary

The devotions to the Seven Sorrows and Seven Joys of the Blessed Virgin Mary are two of the oldest and most beautiful ways of meditating on her interior life. The Sorrows remind us that Our Lady shared deeply in the Passion of her Son, while the Joys remind us of the triumphs and consolations God granted her in return. Together, they reveal the mystery of a heart perfectly united to Jesus in suffering and in glory.

The devotion to the Seven Sorrows grew particularly through the Servite Order in the 13th century, who promoted meditation on the Sorrows as a means of uniting our own sufferings to hers. Later, Franciscan tradition popularized the Seven Joys, known as the Franciscan Crown, as a way of contemplating the other side of Mary's life—the deep joys that flow from faith and perfect love of God.

In both, we learn that holiness is found not in avoiding suffering, but in allowing suffering to be transformed by love. Mary teaches us how to do this with grace, peace, and unshakable trust.

The Seven Sorrows of Mary

1. **The Prophecy of Simeon (Luke 2: 34–35)**
   When Mary and Joseph presented the Child Jesus in the Temple, Simeon prophesied that He would be a "sign of contradiction" and that a sword would pierce her soul. This was Mary's first sorrow—the foreknowledge that her Son was born to suffer. We can imitate her by accepting that love often brings pain, and by offering our own trials for the salvation of souls.

2. **The Flight into Egypt (Matthew 2:13–15)**
   Warned by an angel, Joseph fled with Mary and the Christ Child into Egypt to escape Herod's massacre of the Holy Innocents. Mary suffered the pain of exile and uncertainty, but she trusted completely in God's providence. We imitate her when we face life's disruptions with faith instead of fear, knowing that
   God guides even in the dark.

3. **The Loss of the Child Jesus in the Temple (Luke 2:46–48)**
   After three days of searching, Mary and Joseph found Jesus teaching in the Temple. This sorrow reveals the anguish of losing the presence of God, even temporarily. We imitate Mary when we seek Christ earnestly whenever we lose sight of Him through
   distraction or sin.

4. **Mary Meets Jesus Carrying the Cross (Luke 23:27–31)**
   On the road to Calvary, Mary met her Son bloodied in the midst of His Passion. Her heart broke in silent union with His. We imitate her when we stay near those who suffer, even when we can do nothing but offer our presence and compassion, and when we unite

our sufferings to Christ's.

5. **The Crucifixion and Death of Jesus (John 19:25–27)**
   Mary stood at the foot of the Cross as Jesus gave His life for the world. She offered her Son and herself completely to the will of God. We imitate her when we unite our own crosses to Christ's redemptive love,
   offering them for others.

6. **The Body of Jesus is Placed in Mary's Arms (John 19:38–40)**
   When Jesus was taken down from the Cross, He was laid in His Mother's arms. Her sorrow was unspeakable, yet she received His lifeless body with reverence and love. This is beautifully represented in the sculpture, the *Pietà*. We imitate her when we accept our sufferings as occasions to embrace Christ more deeply.

7. **The Burial of Jesus (John 19:41–42)**
   Mary watched as the stone was rolled before the tomb. She experienced the darkness of separation and loss, yet her faith did not waver. We imitate her when we wait in hope through seasons of silence, trusting that God always brings resurrection.

The Seven Joys of Mary

1. **The Annunciation (Luke 1:28–31)**
   The angel's greeting—"Hail, full of grace"—marked the moment when Heaven bent low to earth. Mary's joy was in doing God's will perfectly. We imitate her joy when we surrender our plans and allow God to
   work through us.

2. **The Visitation (Luke 1:41–45)**
   Mary brought Jesus to Elizabeth, and the infant John leapt in the womb. Her joy was in serving and sharing the presence of Christ. We imitate her when we bring joy and encouragement to others through acts of charity, and when we pray for others to encounter Christ.

3. **The Nativity of Our Lord (Luke 2:6–7)**
   Mary's joy overflowed as she beheld the face of the newborn Christ. In the poverty of Bethlehem, she saw the riches of divine love. We imitate her when we find joy not in comfort or wealth, but in the presence of God among us.

4. **The Adoration of the Magi (Matthew 2:11)**
   When the wise men adored the Child and offered their gifts, Mary rejoiced that her Son was recognized as King and Savior. We imitate her when we acknowledge Christ as Lord in every area of our lives.

5. **The Finding of Jesus in the Temple (Luke 2:46–49)**
   After sorrow came joy. Finding Jesus among the teachers, Mary experienced the peace of reunion and understanding. We imitate her when we persevere in prayer until we rediscover Christ's presence in our lives.

6. **The Resurrection (Matthew 28:6)**
   Mary's faith never failed, but her joy overflowed when her Son rose from the dead. We imitate her joy by living in the light of Easter—believing that no suffering is beyond God's power to redeem.

7. **The Assumption and Coronation of Mary (Psalm 132:8, Revelation 12:1)**
   At the end of her earthly life, Mary was taken body and soul into Heaven and crowned Queen of Heaven and Earth. Her joy was complete in union with God forever. We imitate her by living for Heaven, knowing that our true home is with God.

Reflection

Mary's life was the proper ordering of sorrow and joy, because both were offered entirely to God. In her, suffering is transfigured, and joy is sanctified. When we meditate on her Sorrows and Joys, we begin to see our own lives through the same lens—trusting that every cross leads to glory when accepted with love, and that every tear will be turned to joy with God's grace.

- Take a moment to meditate on one of the Sorrows of Mary. How does this Sorrow relate to my life at this moment?
- Take a moment to meditate on one of the Joys of Mary. How does this Joy relate to my life at this moment?

After the Reflection, pray the Marian Prayers the *Sub Tuum Præsidium*, the *Hail Mary*, and the *Hail Holy Queen.*

The Chaplet of the Seven Sorrows may be found on the Immaculata Institute Podcast "*Word to Your Mother.*"

Day 30

Our Lady of Mount Carmel and the Brown Scapular

"If you wear a scapular or a medal of the Blessed Virgin on your chest and kiss it with gratitude and reverence, then she remembers this act of reverence and love, and for the whole day guides your intelligence and dispels from you more serious temptations."[17]

–St. Maximilian Kolbe

Among the most beloved Marian devotions in the Church is the Brown Scapular of Our Lady of Mount Carmel. It is the original scapular from which so many others have come. The Scapular stands as both a sign and a promise—a sign of belonging to Mary and a promise of her maternal protection at the hour of death.

---

[17] Maximilian Kolbe, "1062 On the Occasion of the Feast of Our Lady of Mount Carmel," in *The Writings of St. Maximilian Maria Kolbe*, vol. 2, *Various Writings* (Lugano, Italy: Nerbini International, 2016), 1880.

The Story of St. Simon Stock

The Scapular devotion began in the 13th century with St. Simon Stock, Prior General of the Carmelite Order. The Carmelite Order had originated on Mount Carmel in the Holy Land, where hermits lived lives of prayer and solitude in honor of the Blessed Virgin Mary. Due to the Muslim reconquest of the Holy Land, it became unsafe for the Carmelites to remain there, forcing them to flee to Europe. There they faced many trials. In the midst of these struggles, St. Simon prayed fervently for Mary's help and protection, and for a sign of her maternal care and patronage over the order.

In 1251, the Blessed Virgin appeared to him surrounded by angels, holding the brown woolen scapular of the Carmelite habit. She said:

> "Receive, My beloved son, this habit of thy order: this shall be to thee and to all Carmelites a privilege, that whosoever dies clothed in this shall never suffer eternal fire .... It shall be a sign of salvation, a protection in danger, and a pledge of peace."

This promise expresses Our Lady's assurance of her intercession, particularly at the hour of death, for those who wear the Scapular faithfully and live in a state of grace.

The Meaning of the Scapular

The word scapular comes from scapula, meaning "shoulder" in Latin. It consists of two small pieces of brown wool connected by strings and worn over the shoulders—one patch on the chest and one on the back. It symbolizes both the Carmelite habit and the yoke of service to Christ through Mary.

To wear the Scapular is to place oneself under Mary's mantle and to live as her faithful servant and disciple. For those who are not members of the Carmelite Order, wearing the Brown Scapular is wearing the *little habit* of the Carmelites—embracing their devotion to Mary. We honor this habit through prayer and thereby dispose ourselves to Mary's promises of her maternal care.

Sacramentals and Grace

The Brown Scapular is a sacramental, not a Sacrament. Sacramentals don't confer grace on their own but dispose us to receive grace through faith and prayer. They are outward signs that remind us of spiritual realities, rather than efficacious signs like the Sacraments (which actually give us the grace they signify). Because we are bodily creatures, physical things—water, oil, the rosary beads, or a small piece of cloth—help us connect to God's invisible grace.

The Scapular embodies the incarnational principle: God works through matter, and Mary, as Mediatrix of grace, intercedes for us in concrete ways—that is, these physical means help dispose us to the grace she obtains for us.

As *Lumen Gentium* teaches, Mary continues to bring us the gifts of eternal life through her maternal care. The Church reminds us not to treat religious symbols as charms, but as signs that point us toward holiness.

The Promises of the Scapular

Mary's promise to St. Simon Stock: "Whoever dies clothed in this shall not suffer eternal fire," must be understood correctly. It is not automatic salvation, but a pledge of her intercession for those who live in grace, strive for chastity according to their state in life, and faithfully follow Christ.

For those who faithfully live the devotion of the Scapular (praying the Rosary, or at least a Hail Mary daily, consecrating oneself to Mary without reserve), she promises her special intercession at the hour of our death, particularly for the grace of final perseverance (remaining faithful to God and in a state of grace until the moment of death).

Tradition also speaks of the Sabbatine Privilege: that those who wear the Scapular devoutly and remain faithful to prayer and virtue will be released from Purgatory on the first Saturday after death. Whether understood literally or spiritually, this promise testifies to Mary's care for souls and her aid to the suffering, both on earth and in Purgatory. It is said in this tradition that Our Lady visits the souls in Purgatory each Saturday, offering some relief to their sufferings.

Devotion and Living the Scapular

The Scapular is more than a garment; it is a way of life. It represents a personal consecration to Mary, a sign that we belong to her and desire to imitate her virtues. To wear it fruitfully, one must live a life of prayer, participate in the Sacraments, and strive for holiness. The Church encourages those enrolled in the Scapular to pray the Rosary daily or to practice regular Marian devotion.

Reflection

Mary's role through the Brown Scapular reminds us that our relationship with her unites us more deeply to the whole Church—the faithful on earth, the souls in Purgatory, and the saints in Heaven. She comforts the suffering and leads all her children to her Son.

To wear the Scapular devoutly is to quietly proclaim: "I am yours, Mary." It is a simple sign of faith and trust—a pledge of belonging and a reminder that, through her intercession, we are never alone on the road to eternal life.

- Do I properly understand that sacramentals require a spiritual devotion?
- How can I correctly utilize sacramentals like the Brown Scapular to deepen my devotion to Mary, and thus grow closer to her Son?

After the Reflection, pray the Marian Prayers the *Sub Tuum Præsidium*, the *Hail Mary*, and the *Hail Holy Queen*.

Day 31

The Miraculous Medal

"Then the Most Blessed Virgin told me: 'The rays you see emanating from the palms of my hands are the symbol of the graces that I bestow on all those who ask me for them,' and with that she gave me to understand how great her generosity is to those who turn to her... How many graces she grants to all those who call upon her!... At that point I lost consciousness, fully absorbed in bliss... Then the Most Blessed Virgin, whose hands were pointing to the ground, was encircled by what looked like an oval frame, on which appeared the following inscription in letters of gold: 'O Mary, conceived without sin, pray for us who have recourse to thee.'

"Then I heard a voice saying to me: 'Have a medal struck according to this model: all those who wear it will receive great graces, especially if they wear it

around their necks. I shall bestow many graces on those who put their trust in me.'"[18]

—St. Catherine Labouré

In 1830, the Blessed Virgin Mary appeared to a young novice of the Sisters of Charity, St. Catherine Labouré, at 140 Rue du Bac in Paris. Through these apparitions, Our Lady gave the Church one of her greatest sacramentals—the Miraculous Medal, a visible sign of her love, intercession, and closeness to her children. This moment marked the beginning of what many call the Age of Mary, when she would appear again and again to call the world to faith and conversion, to prayer and repentance.

The Apparition

On the night of July 18, 1830, Catherine was awakened by a young boy of about five or six (whom she later believed to be her guardian angel) who told her, "The Blessed Virgin is waiting for you." She followed him to the chapel, where she found all the candles lit and the Virgin seated beside the altar. Our Lady spoke to her lovingly, telling her that God wished to entrust her with a mission that would bring both suffering and grace.

Months later, on November 27, during evening meditation, Catherine again saw the Blessed Mother standing on a globe, rays of light streaming from jeweled rings on her fingers. Under her feet was a serpent, crushed beneath her heel—the image of Mary's victory foretold in Genesis 3:15. Around her were the words written in gold:

---

[18] As recounted by Maximilian Kolbe, "1042," in *The Writings of St. Maximilian Maria Kolbe*, vol. 2, *Various Writings* (Lugano, Italy: Nerbini International, 2016), 1851.

"O Mary, conceived without sin, pray for us who have recourse to thee."

Mary explained that the rays of light represented the graces she poured out upon the world—and that the gems which did not shine represented the graces for which people neglected to ask. Then the image turned, revealing an "M" intertwined with a cross, resting above the Sacred Heart of Jesus, crowned with thorns, and the Immaculate Heart of Mary, pierced with a sword. Surrounding it were twelve stars, symbols of her Queenship as Queen Mother of the entire Church (cf. Revelation 12:1).

Mary said simply: "Have a medal struck after this model. All who wear it will receive great graces, especially if they wear it around their necks."

The Medal's Meaning

Every part of the medal expresses a mystery of faith. Mary's foot crushing the serpent reveals her participation in Christ's victory over sin as the one who has enmity with the serpent (cf. Genesis 3:15), who defeats the infernal serpent (cf. Revelation 12). The rays flowing from her hands show her as the Mediatrix of grace, through whom God's mercy reaches the world. The words reference her Immaculate Conception, a truth the Church had in her tradition, but would not formally dogmatically define for another 24 years. The cross rising from the "M" signifies Mary's union with her Son's redemptive work, and the two hearts beneath it express the intimate love of Jesus and Mary—their shared compassion and suffering for souls. The twelve stars remind us that she reigns as Queen of

Heaven, mothering the Church and interceding for all her children.

The Medal and Its Promises

The first medals were struck in 1832, and reports of healings and conversions followed immediately. The devotion spread rapidly, and the faithful soon called it "miraculous" giving it its name, the *Miraculous Medal.* Four years later, the Church declared the apparition authentic.

The Miraculous Medal is a sacramental—a physical sign that disposes us to receive God's grace. It does not have power of its own, but Our Lady blesses those who honor it according to her instruction. To wear it devoutly is to express confidence in Mary's intercession and to remain open to the graces God wishes to give through her. Countless souls have been converted through this devotion, as well as countless others who have witnessed miracles.

A Call to Consecration

The Miraculous Medal is more than a medal—it is a message. It reminds us that Mary is near, that she still crushes the serpent under her feet, and that her intercession is abundant for those who ask. Her hands are never still; the rays of grace continue flow to every soul who turns to her with trust.

Wearing the medal can be a small yet profound act of Marian consecration—a daily reminder that we belong to her and that she leads us always to Christ. St. Maximilian Kolbe required members of the Militia Immaculata to wear the Miraculous Medal as an outward sign of their Marian consecration, saying they "use that medal as a 'bullet' in their fight to win over souls to the Immaculata, confident that the more sincerely and deeply the reign of the Immaculata takes possession of this world, the more this world shall turn into a paradise on earth."[19]

Reflection

Mary's promise still stands: "Great graces will come to all who wear it with faith." May we live each day in the confidence that she is with us—our Mother, our Queen, and our surest path to the Heart of Jesus.

- St. Catherine Labouré prayed fervently to see the Virgin Mary during her lifetime, and it led to one of the greatest gifts to the Church. How can I pray to encounter Our Lady in my life?
- What is keeping me from praying to Our Lady with confidence and boldness? How can I change that today?

After the Reflection, pray the Marian Prayers the *Sub Tuum Præsidium*, the *Hail Mary*, and the *Hail Holy Queen.*

[19] Maximilian Kolbe, "1046 About the Militia of the Immaculata," in *The Writings of St. Maximilian Maria Kolbe*, vol. 2, *Various Writings* (Lugano, Italy: Nerbini International, 2016), 1856.

Day 32

As Soon as Possible, As Soon as Possible, As Soon as Possible

"When the fire of love is ablaze, it cannot be constrained within the heart, but blazes forth and burns, consumes and absorbs other hearts. It conquers more and more souls over to its ideal, to the Immaculata. The Militia of the Immaculata focuses on such love, which goes so far as to win the hearts of all those who live in the present and who will live in the future, and that as soon as possible, as soon as possible, as soon as possible."[20]

–St. Maximilian Kolbe

For St. Maximilian Kolbe, the response to his budding Marian devotion was a sense of urgency. He knew that to give

[20] Maximilian Kolbe, "1224 The Immaculata," in *The Writings of St. Maximilian Maria Kolbe*, vol. 2, *Various Writings* (Lugano, Italy: Nerbini International, 2016), 2121–2122.

his entire life—every moment in the present, and every moment to come in the future—to the Immaculata through a total, radical consecration to her meant that he had a mission to do, which could not wait. In many of his writings, we see this urgency represented in the words, "as soon as possible, as soon as possible, as soon as possible."

To be set aflame with the fire of God's love through Marian consecration brings the necessary effect of blazing forth outwardly. The love received from God through the Immaculata is so strong that it cannot be contained within us, but flows outwardly, just as when Mary visited Elizabeth and John the Baptist in the womb, who experienced the presence of God immediately at the sound of her greeting (cf. Luke 1:41–44).

Kolbe's words emphasize that we must willfully cooperate with these graces so that we might become instruments in Mary's immaculate hands. We undertake the mission of spreading devotion to the Immaculata to extend the Blessed Kingdom of the Most Sacred Heart of Jesus as far as possible, as soon as possible, until every soul who exists in the present and who will ever exist in the future is consecrated to her, and by effect, perfectly belongs to Jesus.

When Will it Happen?

Kolbe's confidence in the Immaculata and her joint mission with the Holy Spirit was so bold that he did not so much wonder *if* this devotion could be spread throughout the world, but *when*:

> When will every living soul throughout the entire globe experience your heart's goodness and love? When will every soul requite you with

> ardent love—made not only of a fleeting feeling—through a complete surrender of the will to you, so that you may rule in the hearts of everybody and form every single heart in the imitation of the Most Sacred Heart of Jesus your divine Son, giving them happiness, and making them godly?[21]

The whole world needs the Immaculata because it needs Jesus. So many people do not receive the precious graces and divine assistance they need because they do not ask for it, have some obstacle to receiving it, or do not even know to ask. Jesus and Mary wait for us to present opportunities to them so that they may give us grace. Out of respect for our free will, they do not force themselves on us, but wait for even the smallest opening of our hearts to come to our aid (and they give us graces to open our hearts, which we must accept and respond to!). Kolbe continues that we have an urgent role in assisting others:

> When will all of this happen?...
>
> Let us commit ourselves to hasten this moment: first and foremost by allowing the Immaculata to take entire possession of our heart so that by becoming instruments in her immaculate hands we will gain, to the limit of our possibilities, the greatest possible number of souls for her, through prayer, through the offering of our sufferings, and work.

---

[21] Maximilian Kolbe, "1159 When Will It Happen?...," in *The Writings of St. Maximilian Maria Kolbe*, vol. 2, *Various Writings* (Lugano, Italy: Nerbini International, 2016), 2009.

> How peaceful and happy we will be on our deathbed at the thought that we
> have endured much fatigue and suffering for love of the Immaculata...[22]

This is the essence of the spiritual battle of which we are a part. It is a battle for souls. Marian consecration is the means by which we take up arms under Mary's banner and mantle of protection, allowing her to crush the head of the serpent through us, destroying all heresies, and leading others to the Truth.

The Whole World and Every Single Soul

Kolbe was greatly influenced by the words of Our Lady at different apparitions. As we have discussed, the words of Our Lady of Lourdes, "I am the Immaculate Conception," fed Kolbe's contemplation on Mary's identity. Likewise, at Rue de Bac, when Our Lady revealed the Miraculous Medal, she said, "The globe that you see stands for the entire world and every single person." These words set the parameters for the Militia Immaculatae and, as such, should be the standard for all those consecrated to Mary: "the entire world and every single person."

"The entire world" because the mediation of the Immaculata is universal, and as such, this devotion must be spread to the ends of the earth to provide to surest path to Jesus. "Every single person" because we are all unique individuals created by God who individually must be saved. By this inspiration, Kolbe said:

---

[22] Ibid.

> *To achieve the goal of the MI as soon as possible,* namely, to win the *whole* world and *every single* soul who now lives or will live until the end of the world for the Immaculata, and through her for the Most Sacred Heart of Jesus.[23]

Reflection

This is our ideal: to consecrate ourselves completely to the Immaculata, uniting our hearts to her Immaculate Heart and the Most Sacred Heart of Jesus, through which we yearn for this love to go out throughout the world, consuming every soul. The essential effect of Marian consecration is transformation in holiness, which necessarily leads to evangelization.

- How can I spread Marian devotion, particularly Marian consecration, in my life, to extend the Blessed Kingdom of the Most Sacred Heart of Jesus?
- What is keeping me from setting my goal as winning the entire universe and the hearts of every person for the Immaculata?

After the Reflection, pray the Marian Prayers the *Sub Tuum Præsidium,* the *Hail Mary,* and the *Hail Holy Queen.*

---

[23] Maximilian Kolbe, "991 Daily Notes, Notebook IV (1930–1933)," in *The Writings of St. Maximilian Maria Kolbe*, vol. 2, *Various Writings* (Lugano, Italy: Nerbini International, 2016), 1757.

Day 33

Living Marian Consecration

"After being inflamed ourselves with this divine love…, we will set the whole world on fire.

However, it is we who have to be inflamed, who should not be lukewarm, but be always ablaze. We have to be merged, to be one with God, through the Immaculata.

We have therefore to concentrate all our attention in this, and solely in this:
to become one, merged solely with the hand of our Teacher and Guide, so that she can do whatever she likes with us."[24]

–St. Maximilian Kolbe

Marian consecration is not a one-time event—it is a way of life, and it is the fruit of *true devotion* to Mary. The act of consecration is only the beginning; living it day by day is what

[24] Maximilian Kolbe, "1160 Our War," in *The Writings of St. Maximilian Maria Kolbe*, vol. 2, *Various Writings* (Lugano, Italy: Nerbini International, 2016), 2011.

transforms us. Each morning, we renew our "yes" to God through the hands of Mary. We remind ourselves that we belong entirely to her, and through her, entirely to Christ.

As Kolbe stated above, we must be inflamed—we must not be lukewarm, but ablaze with God's love through the Immaculata. This consecration is no small thing that can be done half-heartedly, but requires a serious assent of the will done in love for God and the Immaculata, which leads to greater love for souls.

The Essence of Marian Consecration

We recall that Marian consecration is, at its heart, a renewal of our baptismal promises. At baptism, we reject sin and profess our faith in Christ. Through Marian consecration, we continuously live and seek to deepen that reality by intentionally living out our baptismal promises. We entrust ourselves completely to the one who was most perfectly consecrated to God, asking her to help us do what she did: to live for Christ in everything.

When we give ourselves entirely to Mary, we are not replacing our relationship with Jesus—we are allowing her to bring us into it more perfectly. God chose to come to us through her; we choose to return to Him the same way, through the one whose soul magnifies the Lord (cf. Luke 1:46).

Living Marian Consecration

When we make a true consecration to Mary, it is like entering through a threshold. We are no longer our own; we no longer seek to manage our own spiritual lives, but entrust everything into her hands. We belong more perfectly to Jesus through her, because she takes all of our merits, our prayers, our good works, and offers them to her Son as her own on our behalf.

The Immaculata makes our gifts more immaculate, transforming them into suitable offerings to Christ, and obtains for us countless graces for our salvation and even our temporal needs—all ordered toward deepening our relationship with Christ and making us holy. As such, our consecration must become the lens through which we view all things.

It is appropriate to daily seek to do the Immaculata's will because it is in perfect union with God's will. This will not obscure our intentions to become conformed to the Most Sacred Heart of Jesus, but will strengthen them. We must acknowledge, though, that we are merely human, and have a finite attention span. It is to be expected that we will struggle to keep Jesus and the Immaculata in the forefront of our minds at every waking moment; therefore, we must regularly renew this consecration to Mary.

A formal renewal of consecration should happen at least once per year—but I recommend much more frequently. One would certainly not lose any benefit by continuously going through formal preparations for consecration. I would at least do so a few times a year. Also, as I regularly recommend: if you are ready to consecrate yourself to Mary, make an act of the will immediately. Do not delay (as soon as possible, as soon as possible, as soon as possible). Once you are done with your preparation, that act of consecration will only have *deeper meaning*.

With this in mind, it would be incomprehensibly profitable to say a prayer of total consecration to Mary every single day, whether a formal prayer (such as those by St. Louis de Montfort or St. Maximilian Kolbe) or one from the heart.

Daily Marian Devotions

To live our consecration, we have to cultivate a daily relationship with Our Lady. It is not complicated, but must be consistent. We would do well to remember a few examples that we have spoken of throughout these days of coming to know the Immaculata together:

- The Rosary—The Rosary is the school of Mary. Through it, she teaches us the mysteries of Christ's life and forms our interior gaze to be like hers—always fixed on Jesus. We might also pray the Chaplet of the Seven Sorrows or the Franciscan Crown Rosary (of the Seven Joys of Mary).
- The Brown Scapular—The Scapular is a sign of belonging to Mary—an outward expression of our consecration. It also helps us to keep in mind Mary's maternal protection and intercession in our lives. We honor it by praying the Rosary, the Little Office of the Blessed Virgin Mary, or at least by the recitation of the Hail Mary.
- The Miraculous Medal — This medal given directly by Mary calls us to pray, "O Mary, conceived without sin, pray for us who have recourse to thee."
- The First Saturdays—A devotion of reparation to her Immaculate Heart. Confession, Communion, the Rosary, and meditation—done in love—consoles her heart and deepens our union with hers.
- Prayer from the Heart—We ought to pray from our hearts in spontaneous conversation with the Immaculata daily. She loves us as a Mother, and

wants to speak to her children. Don't forget to call your Mother!

Reflection

The goal of this life of consecration is union with Christ. The more faithfully we live it, the more our hearts become conformed to His Sacred Heart through hers. This is the "secret" of the saints—whereby she transforms us into the image of her Son. She transforms our ordinary moments into opportunities for grace. Our work, our family life, our struggles—all of it becomes part of her mission to bring souls to Jesus. Living Marian consecration unites us more deeply with the Church—on earth, in purgatory, and in heaven—because Mary's motherhood extends to every member of Christ's Body.

When we live our consecration, we are not just privately devoted to Mary. We are enlisted under her banner, cooperating with her in the work of redemption, helping souls come to know and love her Son.

- What change will I make today to more faithfully live a total consecration to Mary?
- What devotional practices can I realistically integrate into my daily routine today (so that I stick with them long-term)?

After the Reflection, pray the Marian Prayers the *Sub Tuum Præsidium*, the *Hail Mary*, and the *Hail Holy Queen*.

Consecration Day

On the date of total consecration to the Immaculata, one should attend Mass is possible. Additionally, one should go to Confession (or at least go to Confession within a few days before making the act of total consecration). The Rosary should be recited, during which one places oneself in the presence of Jesus and Mary.

Following the Rosary, the *Sub Tuum Præsidium* may be said, before concluding with the Consecration Prayer of St. Maximilian Kolbe:

> O Immaculata, Queen of Heaven and earth, refuge of sinners and our most loving Mother, God has willed to entrust the entire order of mercy to you. I, a repentant sinner, cast myself at your feet, humbly imploring you to take me with all that I am and have, wholly to yourself as your possession and property. Please make of me, of all my powers of soul and body, of my whole life, death and eternity, whatever most pleases you.

If it pleases you, use all that I am and have without reserve, wholly to accomplish what was said of you: 'She will crush your head' [Gn 3:15], and 'You alone have destroyed all heresies in the whole world' [Office of the B.V. Mary]. Let me be a fit instrument in your immaculate and merciful hands for introducing and increasing your glory to the maximum in all the many strayed and indifferent souls, and thus help extend as far as possible the blessed kingdom of the Most Sacred Heart of Jesus. For wherever you enter you obtain the grace of conversion and growth in holiness, since it is through your hands that all graces come to us from the Most Sacred Heart of Jesus.

V. Allow me to praise you, O Sacred Virgin.
R. Give me strength against your enemies.

Marian Prayers

Sub Tuum Præsidium

We fly to thy protection,
O holy Mother of God.
Despise not our petitions in our necessities,
but deliver us always from all dangers,
O glorious and blessed Virgin.

Hail Mary

Hail Mary, full of grace, the Lord is with thee.
Blessed art thou among women,
and blessed is the fruit of thy womb, Jesus.
Holy Mary, Mother of God,
prayer for us sinners now and at the hour of our death. Amen.

Hail, Holy Queen

Hail, Holy Queen, Mother of Mercy,
our life, our sweetness and our hope.
To you do we cry,
poor banished children of Eve.
To you do we send up our sighs,
mourning and weeping in this valley of tears
Turn then, most gracious advocate,
your eyes of mercy toward us,
and after this exile
show unto us the blessed fruit of thy womb,
Jesus.

O clement, O loving,
O sweet Virgin Mary.
Pray for us, O Holy Mother of God
That we may be made worthy of the promises of Christ.
Amen.

Consecration Prayer of St. Maximilian Kolbe

O Immaculata, Queen of Heaven and earth, refuge of sinners and our most loving Mother, God has willed to entrust the entire order of mercy to you. I, a repentant sinner, cast myself at your feet, humbly imploring you to take me with all that I am and have, wholly to yourself as your possession and property. Please make of me, of all my powers of soul and body, of my whole life, death and eternity, whatever most pleases you.

If it pleases you, use all that I am and have without reserve, wholly to accomplish what was said of you: 'She will crush your head' [Gn 3:15], and 'You alone have destroyed all heresies in the whole world' [Office of the B.V. Mary]. Let me be a fit instrument in your immaculate and merciful hands for introducing and increasing your glory to the maximum in all the many strayed and indifferent souls, and thus help extend as far as possible the blessed kingdom of the Most Sacred Heart of Jesus.

For wherever you enter you obtain the grace of conversion and growth in holiness, since it is through your hands that all graces come to us from the Most Sacred Heart of Jesus.

V. Allow me to praise you, O Sacred Virgin.
R. Give me strength against your enemies.

About the Author

Joshua Mazrin is a Catholic speaker and writer whose specialties include the Blessed Virgin Mary, St. Maximilian Kolbe, the Immaculata, and prayer. Mazrin directed an apostolate in the Diocese of Brooklyn and served as the Director of Evangelization for the Diocese of Venice in Florida. He is a graduate of the Franciscan University of Steubenville where he earned both a bachelor's and master's degree in theology.

Mazrin has also led both for and nonprofit corporations including work in real estate development, publishing, and higher education.

He also the Founder and Executive Director of The Immaculata Institute, a 501(c)(3) nonprofit dedicated to extending the mission of St. Maximilian Kolbe to win the entire universe over to the Immaculata, and thus extend the Blessed Kingdom of the Most Sacred Heart of Jesus as far as possible, "and all this as soon as possible, as soon as possible, as soon as possible."

Fr. Matthias M. Sasko, FI is a Franciscan Friar of the Immaculate and author of *Preparation for Total Consecration to the Immaculate according to St. Maximilian M. Kolbe.*

www.ingramcontent.com/pod-product-compliance
Lightning Source LLC
LaVergne TN
LVHW090604110826
845146LV00001B/257

* 9 7 9 8 9 9 4 7 7 3 9 2 5 *